D1426338

SCOTLAND

Land of Mountains

Clydesdale Bank PLC

ACKNOWLEDGEMENTS

The publisher gratefully acknowledges copyright permission granted from the following sources for the right to reproduce quotations in *Scotland - Land of Mountains*:

Nan Shepherd (*The Living Mountain*), J. Morton Boyd (*The Highlands and Islands*), John Prebble and Martin Secker & Warburg Ltd (*John Prebble's Scotland*), Allan Campbell McLean and Highlands and Islands Enterprise (*Explore the Highlands and Islands*), Eric Robinson and Curtis Brown Ltd (John Clare's *A Song*), Magnus Magnusson (*The Nature of Scotland*), Maimie Nethersole-Thompson and Adam Watson (*The Cairngorms*), and W. H. Murray (*Mountaineering in Scotland*).

We are very grateful to the following: Magnus Magnusson for the foreword; Dr Roddy Fairley, Dr Derek Ratcliffe, Dr Adam Watson, Dr David Horsfield, John Mackay, Dr Philip Whitfield, Dr Bob Aitken, Alan Brown, Alan McKirdy, Dr John Gordon, Dr Ingvar Byrkjedal, Dr Pat Thompson, Dr Paul Haworth, Dr Stuart Rae, Professor Michael B. Usher, Professor Roger Crofts and Maimie Nethersole-Thompson for comments or advice; Dr John M. Francis for first bringing us together; and Scottish Natural Heritage and the Clydesdale Bank for sponsoring the book. The views expressed herein are entirely ours, and should not be read as SNH policy.

First published in 1995 by
Colin Baxter Photography Ltd
Grantown-on-Spey
Morayshire
Reprinted 1996

A CIP catalogue record for this book is available from the British Library

ISBN 0-948661-61-5

Front Cover Photograph: THE BLACK CUILLIN, ISLE OF SKYE
Back Cover Photograph: GLENCOE FROM THE AIR

Printed in Hong Kong

SCOTLAND

Land of Mountains

Colin Baxter & Des Thompson

Colin Baxter Photography, Grantown-on-Spey, Scotland

Contents

Foreword

Whatever there may be of greatness in a man's mind will grow and go out in sympathy with the greatness of the mountain world: whatever is little will shrink. So that where one man is intimidated another is ennobled.

W. H. Murray, *Mountaineering in Scotland*, 1947 (revised 1962)

On the wall of my room there hangs a Landsat map of Scotland: a snapshot from space of that very special part of planet earth we call Scotland. From that viewpoint in space we catch glimpses of extraordinary richness and variety – the Southern Uplands, Breadalbane, the Grampians, the North-West Highlands and the myriad Northern and Western Isles, all set in a giant jigsaw of mountain, moorland and sea.

I use the quotation from Bill Murray's *Mountaineering in Scotland* at the head of this foreword because it is a down-to-earth book which captures so much of the fascination and the veneration which Scotland's mountains hold for people. And it is totally apt that the thoughts he articulated in that quotation were inspired on the great top of Cairn Toul – just before a blizzard which almost killed him and his companions. His book is a classic of mountaineering; and this new book is written with the same sense of reverence which informed so much of Bill Murray's work. Here are panoramas and views never seen in print before, an exultant picture gallery of mountains illuminated by a text which does them full justice.

All mountains have their distinct personas. And every mountain has a different aspect, depending, literally, on your standpoint. In Iceland, for instance, where the business of mountain building is by no means complete, a fissure volcano seen from the south can look like a cone volcano from the east – and sometimes even has two names to reflect this difference of perspective.

I never fail to be surprised by the changing nature of mountain personalities: colours, patterns, textures and shapes, all playing directly on the senses and on the imagination. Every time I drive through the Pass of Drumochter, for instance, the landscape wears a different expression – welcoming, yes, but so often brooding, presenting a dark and lowering visage even on the sunniest of days. No one can ever really understand a mountain – not even Bill Murray, that poet of the peaks; but a mountain helps one to understand oneself.

This is not simply 'wilderness' – a term I happen to find unhelpful, because so many of our wild areas are inhabited and managed. 'Wilderness' is a misnomer. But we do have wild landscapes, with the natural elements of rock, water, peat and vegetation so predominant. It is the inhabitation and management (or lack of it) of some of these areas which has meant that wherever one looks there seem to be conflict and difficulty. This is a land which gives to all what it can, but receives sorely little in return.

When we regard this wild country of rock and scree, much depends, I suggest, on perspectives and perceptions. Not just in Scotland but across all Europe, these have changed radically in little more than a couple of centuries. Back in the early 1700s the mountain land was considered forbidding and unattractive – imagine that! In 1726 Daniel Defoe voiced his contempt for the mountainous environment of southern Scotland in his *Tour through the Whole Island of Great Britain*, where he concluded that heath or heather was merely, 'a foil to the beauty of the rest of England'; and David Burt, a Hanoverian officer in General Wade's entourage in the aftermath of the 1715 Rising, described the Highlands in unflattering words: 'The summits of the Highest Mountains are mostly destitute of Earth, and the huge naked Rocks, being just above the heath, produce the disagreeable Appearance of a scabbed Head.' But not long after Burt penned these words, and while others (such as Dr Johnson in his *Journey to the Western Islands of Scotland* in 1773) were still taking just such a jaundiced view of the mountains, a

A momentary gap in a white-out – Looking towards Ben Macdui, Cairngorms (opposite).

more romantic regard for the wild places was being born in the hearts and minds of the Lakeland poets such as Wordsworth. In Scotland itself, Walter Scott's writings heralded an important change – a link between wild land and patriotism which epitomised his historically romantic ardour in *The Lay of the Last Minstrel* (1805):

O Caledonia! stern and wild,
Meet nurse for a poetic child!
Land of brown heath and shaggy wood,
Land of the mountain and the flood,
Land of my Sires! what mortal hand
Can e'er untie the filial band
That knits me to thy rugged strand!

But it is in *The Lord of the Isles* (1815) that Scott gave his enthusiasm most florid expression, on the Road to the Isles between Glencoe and Skye:

Such are the scenes, where savage grandeur wakes
An awful thrill that softens into sighs;
Such feelings rouse them by dim Rannoch's lakes,
In dark Glencoe such gloomy raptures rise:
Or further, where, beneath the northern skies,
Chides wild Loch-Eribol his caverns hoar
But, be the minstrel judge, they yield the prize
Of desert dignity to that dread shore,
That sees grim Coolin rise and hears Coriskin roar.

The era of the Great Sheep revolutionised the culture and economy of the Highlands and created a new perception of how to make money out of the romance. By the end of the eighteenth century, however, sheep prices were starting to fall and red deer became the new fashion. The Victorian Age capitalised on the romance both of mountains and of red deer in an astonishing outburst of entrepreneurialism, symbolised for all time by Landseer's celebrated *Monarch of the Glen* – an era which has been tellingly dubbed by Sir John Lister-Kaye as 'the Balmorality Epoch'. Deer hunting, once the prerogative only of absolute monarchs, became fashionable throughout the Highlands. Vast baronial shooting lodges were built to accommodate the revival of this sporting passion, where southern industrialists could play at being kings of Scottish castles after a hard day on the hill.

Today the legacy of our uplands is still coloured by these Victorian passions. We have an enormously fragmented estate pattern; we have vast ranges of bare and deer-dotted moorlands which reinforce the idea of scenic grandeur which visitors associated with Scotland – whereas to the ecologist that grandeur hides a perilous biological impoverishment; hillsides once clothed in Caledonian wild-wood, and higher by sub-alpine scrub, are now denuded and scoured by erosion; straths and valleys once verdant are now bitten to the quick by man's beasts – not only sheep but also the rabbits he introduced in Norman times, and the red deer he has allowed to multiply far beyond the capacity of the natural habitat to carry them sustainably in some parts.

In his lecture on 'The Highlands and the Roots of Green Consciousness, 1750-1990' (Scottish Natural Heritage, SNH Occasional Paper 1, 1993), Professor Christopher Smout, the current Historiographer Royal in Scotland and deputy chairman of SNH, brilliantly chronicled the rise of the 'green consciousness' movement and its development into the nature conservation ethos of today. There is now also a growing interest in the history of mountaineering in Scotland, vividly captured by Cameron McNeish and Richard Else in *The Edge: One Hundred Years of Scottish Mountaineering* (BBC Books, 1994).

So today we also have another factor to contend with: more people than ever are seeing the mountain land as haven and sanctuary from the pressures of modern life, and are visiting the mountains in increasing numbers.

One of our tasks in Scottish Natural Heritage is to help people to enjoy the beauty and diversity of the Scottish countryside, and to gain a greater understanding and appreciation of it. Our operational philosophy is clear-cut: we must sustain the natural heritage if we want it to sustain us. If people in Scotland are armed to care for the environment (with the appropriate information, resources, commitment and empowerment) the natural heritage can be sustained. That is why SNH has as its slogan 'Working with Scotland's people to care for our natural heritage'. We have local offices throughout the country with staff developing and implementing conservation-related activities sensitive to the needs of the local people and to the distinctive character of their area.

For most of this century, ideas about nature conservation have centred on the identification and subsequent protection of the rare and the representative – witness the designation of National Nature Reserves, Sites of Special Scientific Interest and indeed Local Nature Reserves. Similarly, ideas about caring for landscapes and the pleasure to be derived from outstanding scenery have led to the designation of National Scenic Areas and the establishment of Regional Parks and Country Parks – a process reflected in the creation of National Parks in many other countries. Today the need for protection and management of special areas remains an important aspect of the conservation of biodiversity and landscape, and of providing for enjoyment of the countryside. Looking to the future, the European Union Directives (on Wild Birds, and on Habitats and Species) will have important implications for the positive management of the natural heritage – and so, too, will the new Scottish designation of Natural Heritage Area (NHA) when it comes about.

However, more and more we are coming to recognise that the safeguarding of special areas is not enough. Nature and its systems do not respect such boundaries. Birds such as golden eagles range widely, and many others are migratory. Pollutants penetrate the remotest and largest of protected areas far from their source. Success in maintaining the diversity of species and the richness of landscape quality in the special areas cannot be achieved without addressing the way in which the rest of the countryside is used and managed. We need to take proper care of wildlife and its habitat everywhere, to have respect for nature in our own backyards as well as in the more spectacular places: all of Scotland is special.

But in the mountains we shall always face some of the toughest challenges. There have been long-standing frictions between estate owners and managers, nature conservationists and the recreationists who wish to enjoy the mountains in a totally untrammelled way. Nevertheless the Cairngorms Working Party, of which I had the privilege to be chairman, found an encouraging desire by all for a way forward based on co-operation, mutual understanding and tolerance. And when, in 1994, SNH published its policy paper on 'Red Deer and the Natural Heritage', the positive response was immensely gratifying.

This is a book by two enthusiasts who view the mountains with freshness and hope. Colin Baxter, renowned photographer and adventurous publisher, has taken superb photographs which grace over twenty marvellous books and literally millions of scenic postcards; the term 'Baxter view' is ascribed by many to special atmospheric panoramas! Ecologist Dr Des Thompson, head of the Uplands and Peatlands Branch of the Research and Advisory Services Directorate in SNH, was set going on the wilds of Sutherland at the age of four by his late father, the naturalist Desmond Nethersole-Thompson; here he unleashes all his stored love and knowledge of our mountain country. Together, photographer and writer have produced a treasury of views, in both senses of the word, which does rich justice to this special land of mountains we call Scotland.

Magnus Magnusson

Magnus Magnusson KBE
Chairman, Scottish Natural Heritage

The Mountains – Past and Present

I can imagine the antiquity of rock, but the antiquity of a living flower – that is harder…

Mankind is sated with noise; but up here, this naked, this elemental savagery, this infinitesimal cross-section of sound from the energies that have been at work for aeons in the universe, exhilarates rather than destroys. Each of the senses is a way into what the mountain has to give.

Nan Shepherd, *The Living Mountain*, 1977

There are two truly wild kingdoms in Scotland – that of the mountains and that of its sea. Across the world almost a third of the land surface is mountainous yet the high ground of Scotland holds a special appeal. Why? Perhaps it is the scenery, the great character of the land, or the myriad of landscapes, plants and animals. It is all of these things, of course, and much more. These places are a living expression of nature and our culture, changing in ways that are dynamic, with roots as much in the great geological epochs as in the tenacious grip of man.

This peerless land of mountains is predominantly bare, largely devoid of natural woodland and scrub, but with a moody, natural beauty. As we move from region to region we are struck by this distinctive range of places, all so accessible and appealing. We pass from the great open bogland expanse of Rannoch Moor to the strong bold features of Glencoe, and then on to Loch Leven, Loch Linnhe and surrounding coastal woods. In the North-West Highlands there are silvery beaches, skerries and sea cliffs next to arctic-alpine heaths, patches of woodland, great bogs and pools pitted in knobbly terrain – all flanked by steep, craggy hulks of mountains. Travel south-east, and in a few hours you are amongst the quiltwork of heather moors, remnants of native pinewood and scattered birchwoods, and above these the great granite massifs with their boulder fields, sheer towering corries and glistening snowbeds.

Many other aspects come to mind, but the scale and variety of this wonderful land is utterly unforgettable.

This is a book about Scotland's mountains, dedicated to their wildness and special appeal. There are four parts: essays on mountain environments and the effects of man, a journey through some key regions, and a final reflection on their significance. It is neither a guide to the Munros and Corbetts nor a celebration of their spiritual wonders. Instead, it is an excursion through this magnificent land, taking a personal look at its nature and ways.

Early Beginnings

Let us start with the formation of mountains. As huge chunks of the earth's crust drift over the globe, growing at literally a few millimetres each year, some collide. We find many stories in the annals of geology about the building of our land. Snapshots of these, stretching back billions of years, reveal a great history of battles involving glaciers, scores of rock types, volcanic eruptions, swamps, deserts, earthquakes, and vast oceans.

Nowhere are the contrasts more compelling than on a journey south from the north of Scotland. One of the oldest rocks in the world, Lewisian gneiss, underlies much of the far north-west Highlands and Outer Isles. The lower ground has millions of rugged, mamillated, banded rocky exposures. Stand on one of these and you are close to rocks created almost at the beginning of time on earth. Around three billion years ago this rock was formed and has, since then, been shoved upwards from the earth's lower crust. But then move down to the southern edge of the Highlands, stand on Ben Lomond, and look down over woody crags to Loch Lomond – the largest freshwater loch in Britain. Here, the final phase of the last Ice Age reached its limit. A huge ice-field smothered much of the central and western Highlands (with

LOCHABER (opposite) "…mountains rise up to be sculptured by the erosive influences of rain, wind, ice and sea."

smaller ice-fields forming on the Grampians, Skye and Mull). As the ice built up, the glaciers poured out into the west coast adding to the ragged sea lochs. Not since then has Britain experienced such a major form of environmental change. Nevertheless, that we can transcend such geological epochs within the space of just a few hour's driving and walking is a marvel peculiar to Scotland.

At the broadest scale, the main mountain regions lie between furrows running from the south-west to the north-east. A good deal of this structural pattern is attributed to the Caledonian mountain-building episode, which occurred about 450 million years ago. And it is at the advent of this time that the mountains, as we see them today, began to form.

Just under 550 million years ago an ocean, which geologists call Iapetus, separated two great continents. One of these had elements of what is now North America, Greenland, Scotland and Northern Ireland; the other was formed from terrain now part of mainland Europe, southern Great Britain and Southern Ireland. The ocean swelled, with lava pouring up through fractures in the ocean floor as the continents drifted apart. But later on, the ocean contracted and its floor disappeared under the intense overriding movements of continents. Massive volcanic eruptions along the continental margins marked this spell and mountains began to emerge. The Iapetus Ocean continued to shrink until, at the end of the Silurian period, the continents collided and mountains rose up to form land. At that time the Scottish Highlands of today were already above the sea, but the Southern Uplands were newly-formed from the mud, sand and volcanic debris deposited in the depths of the Iapetus Ocean.

There followed events over millions of years characterised by great erosion and weathering and, subsequently, inundation by the seas. Early freshwater lochs disappeared and Carboniferous 'coal swamps' formed. Immense volcanic activity, and then desert conditions, afflicted the land. Later, a great flood drowned all but the highest of mountain land. The seas subsided, the earth's crust ripped under yet more volcanic eruptions, and the North Atlantic Ocean formed. A line of volcanoes formed from Arran to Skye, with the Black and Red Cuillin today having wonderful examples of their deep roots. Before we consider the final period of change – the Ice Age – we should first dwell on the geology and division of mountain areas into geological regions.

Rocks and Soils

Geology provides the foundation of life. The rocks give a form and structure to the land, and mineral substance to the soils. The mixture of rock types and their chronology is complex. Rocks are grouped into three types, and each of these has special characteristics.

Igneous rocks vary in composition and are derived from the depths of the earth's crust. Some of these poured out through cracks and craters and included volcanic lavas and ash. Intrusive rocks, as the term implies, have intruded or forced their way into overlying rocks, and include granite, gabbro and pegmatite. **Sedimentary** rocks derive either from the weathered remains of older rocks (such as clays, sandstones, shales, till, greywackes) or from organic origins (coal, limestone). These are more readily aged, and geology maps are multi-coloured recording the distribution of the rocks, ranging from Torridonian Sandstone (800-1,100 million years) and Cambrian limestones and quartzites to the younger Carboniferous (280-350 million years) and Jurassic successions. Finally, there are the **metamorphic** rocks whose composition and structure have been changed radically by pressure and heat. In the Highlands and Islands this is the main rock, and what we take for granted in many areas are the stumps of ancient mountains sliced, eroded and battered by the elements. Gneiss, quartzite, schists and slate are all metamorphic rocks. The advent of Lewisian gneiss goes back almost to 3,000 million years ago, whereas Moine schists are more recent, dating back only a billion years, and the Dalradians are younger still. This detail matters, not only in broadening our appreciation of the heritage of the land, but also because it affects what we see at scales ranging from miles to mere feet.

THE BLACK CUILLIN from inner Loch Bracadale, Isle of Skye – Mountains that encapsulate the history of the land.

THE HIGHLAND BOUNDARY FAULT

The Highland Boundary Fault runs from Helensburgh to Stonehaven.

Above Conic Hill, looking south-west over Loch Lomond, four of the loch's 30 islands lie on the line between the Highlands and the Lowlands. On the right (north) are hard, ancient Dalradian metamorphic rocks of a rugged landscape meeting the younger, softer sandstones of the Devonian age to the south-east.

This Highland Boundary Fault, just over 1km wide in parts, is obvious here because the crushed rocks have resisted weathering. The rocks of the south bore down on the Highland rocks leaving a step-like imprint on the land. The Devonian rocks date from around 550-445 million years ago, and became attached to the Highland block as a result of plate tectonic movements pushing them sideways. The rocks came from part of the floor of a small ocean basin, with the movements between the blocks actually occurring some 420-390 million years ago.

Much more recently, just over 10,000 years ago, Loch Lomond again featured prominently in history – this time giving its name to the Loch Lomond Re-advance. Arctic conditions prevailed widely for the last time – ice built up in the south-west Highlands, advancing into the Lowlands as far south as Alexandria.

At the finest scale, the rocks have a marked influence on the land. The different rock types, so variable across Scotland, have generally clear effects on soil formation, and on associated plants and animals. Most of the rocks are hard and non-calcareous; most of the soils tend towards acidic and podsolised (much of their chemical bases having been leached out). This word 'acidic' needs to be defined clearly given its importance to the sustenance of upland life. Soil acidity is measured according to the pH (potential of Hydrogen) scale, with soils below a pH of 4.5 being acidic, whereas those of pH 6.0-7.0 are more basic (rather than simply neutral).

Peat is the classic acid soil which smothers much of the flatter and more waterlogged upland surfaces. Within this we have compost-heap processes working in reverse. There is so little decomposition of dead plant remains that the surface rises slowly, at something like 2mm per year, with the wet and airless conditions providing acidic conditions for its suite of plants. Peat is a remarkable entity – having fewer solids than milk, and growing out of the protracted life of the dead.

Calcium is the key nutrient base harnessed by plants, and when taken up by the soils from rocks produces a high, basic pH. Calcareous rocks are, however, scarce in Scotland with the richest ones being the Dalradian limestones and calcareous schists in Perthshire, Argyll and a few parts of Angus. The Durness dolomitic limestone in the North-West Highlands is rich in magnesium. Other rocks are fairly basic, such as hornblende schists, local lime-rich bands in Old Red Sandstone and basalts. Most crystalline rocks (except limestone) tend to yield little or no calcium, giving acidic soils, so typical of much of the uplands in Scotland. These tend to be the poorest for mountain plants and grazing animals.

Not all areas with these hard rocks are poor though, for some receive richer material washed down or flushed from higher up, or brought to the surface by bubbling springs from lower, richer seams. We also come upon glacial drift – unsorted materials including boulders and gravel washed out by the melting ice of glaciers – which has in places been dumped many miles from its parent rock to produce poor, infertile conditions, quite often over rich rocks.

Mountain Regions

There are five mountain regions demarcated by a thrust plane or faults: the Southern Uplands, Central Lowlands, Central Highlands, Northern Highlands, and the North-West Highlands.

Between the Southern Uplands Fault and the Scotland-England Border is the smallest region. Here there are regular series of pillow-like hills with many crumples and creases. Glacial erosion here was more limited in its effects than in many other areas of the uplands. The bulk of the rocks are Silurian (400-450 million years old) with a broad band of the older Ordovician along the Fault. In the south-west, there are hard granite masses, and the great ice-scourings have made the Galloway hills more rugged than the rest, creating wierd impressions of being in the western Highlands.

The Central Lowlands, south of the Highland Boundary Fault, have hills rather than mountains. This area is mainly made of Carboniferous and Old Red Sandstone sedimentary rocks, with numerous volcanic features. In general, the area is heavily exploited by man. Mines, quarries, shale bings and the like attest to organic deposits in ancient coal swamps and the debris from great glaciers. Parts of the Pentland Hills, Sidlaws, and the Ochils are volcanic in origin.

The Northern and Central Highland regions lie between the Moine Thrust Plane and the Highland Boundary Fault (with the Great Glen Fault lying between them). The latter stretches diagonally south-west from Stonehaven to the Firth of Clyde and is obvious to anybody who has seen a satellite photograph of Scotland. The Moine Thrust Plane is altogether different. It runs south-westwards from Loch Eriboll to Glen Carron, and through the Sleat Peninsula on Skye. Here Moine schists have been forced westwards, over Lewisian gneiss, Torridonian sandstone and Cambrian quartzite-limestone. Along parts of this thrust slices of limestone became detached and now outcrop as isolated patches

You can readily imagine the power of ice as it carved out the Lairig Ghru in the Cairngorm mountains.

on some mountain tops. Throughout, the rocks are mainly Dalradian (named after the first Scots kingdom, Dalradia) and Moine schists, overlain in the east by younger sedimentary Old Red Sandstone. Towards the east and in the Cairngorms there are the granite plateaux and hills, which are much poorer in nutrients but form Scotland's most extensive, high arctic-like environment.

Finally, there is the north-west Highlands and Islands region – lying west of the Moine Thrust. This extraordinary land has Lewisian Gneiss hills (as high as 760m on Harris) splattered amongst a primaeval lunar-like ice-scoured landscape. The reddish Torridonian rocks overlie much of the gneiss but are actually stalks of even greater mountains long since stripped away by weathering and erosion. The Torridon mountains, such as Beinn Eighe (capped by Cambrian quartzite) and An Teallach, are spectacular members of a weather-beaten group of uniquely attractive natural cathedrals.

On the northern Inner Hebrides we have two kinds of igneous rocks – the extrusive lavas on northern Skye, building the Trotternish Ridge, and the intrusive complexes that give rise to the Rum skyline and the razor sharp ridges and pinnacles of the Black Cuillin on Skye. On Trotternish there is that peculiarly strange construction of cliffs and hills formed by landslips, appreciated at its best when looking over the mystical Quiraing.

Ice and Its Retreat

We return to the continuing changes to the land, and turn specifically to the age of ice, or at least its demise.

As far back as two and a half million years ago northern Europe began to experience the Ice Age. Since then the mountains have had glaciers during at least four major episodes, and during the coldest the whole country was in the grip of ice. Each time glaciers formed the features and deposits of the preceding phase were modified to various degrees. So much of what we understand today, however, concerns the last major glaciation. This began some 115,000 years ago. As the glaciers advanced and receded, vegetated habitats formed and then perished, and even some 106,000 years ago birchwoods formed near Inverness.

This most recent Ice Age reached its zenith only 18,000 years ago, when the expanse of ice was near-continuous. With the probable exception of north-west Lewis, and some of the mountains in the western Highlands and Islands, the whole of Scotland was under ice. Sheltered spots close to the sea in the west may have been missed, but eastwards there was no sea – just ice. Generally, Scotland must have resembled East Greenland today – an ice-locked land with only a few tiny glens, a handful of fairly coastal areas with any stunted vegetation, and mountains near-submerged in ice.

The ice produced the main mountain shapes – with the work of frost action, rivers and gravity adding further to the diversity of land forms. Glaciers gouged out U-shaped glens or glacial troughs, pulverised rocks and spawned huge chunks of ice. With the retreat of ice, river-glens clogged up with boulder clay and sediments, washed out by rivers at the vanguard of the glaciers. Ice-dammed lochs were drained – their ramparts breached – and the shoreline dropped leaving tell-tale strandlines such as the Parallel Roads in Glen Roy. At certain times when the ice sheet was less extensive the exposed land was near-permanently frozen, thawing only briefly in summer as the northern tundra does now. At the height of the glaciation so much water was locked up as ice that the sea-level was around 120m lower than today. Such was the weight of ice that the underlying land compressed, then it rebounded when the ice melted, leaving raised beaches, and where the ice was thickest those parts of Scotland today continue to rise imperceptibly.

Between 13,000 and 12,000 years ago the climate warmed at a rate faster than that recorded from any previous epoch (around 2.8°C per century). There was a cold blip around 11,000 years ago, but again a thousand years later the climate warmed. The giant shroud of ice retreated ever so slowly. As the melt-water's silts, raw soils and shallow lochs were colonised by lower plants, then others, the habitats shifted through ecological succession from tundra to heath, steppe, scrub and finally to forest. The land changed further, with the re-shaping of river valleys, alluvial fans and other present-day features, some of which continue to change and form.

And what dynamism, as these ecosystems advanced and developed gradually northwards, dwindling in diversity and richness in the higher and more isolated reaches. For the plants and animals these were heady times, and the rate of colonisation and expansion must have been nothing short of spectacular. There would have been great mammals then – caribou/reindeer, elk, brown bear and wolves – but not, it seems, mammoth, musk ox and woolly rhinoceros. And amongst the birds there must have been truly arctic breeders – non-existent or scarce in Scotland now – such as long-tailed duck, smew, king eider, snowy owl, gyr falcon, long-tailed skua, broad-billed sandpiper, turnstones, Lapland buntings, bluethroats and arctic redpoll.

Primaeval Habitats

The first woodland was birch and hazel – Scots pine came some 1,500 years later – and the scrub making way for this was mainly of hazel, willow, juniper and birch. It is doubtful that those first hazel woods were so different from those found today on parts of Skye and Mull. Willow and alder colonised over the wetter sites, and later oak came in, eventually to replace pine in the coastal and lower lying reaches towards the south.

Some 8,000-9,000 years ago the summer climate was warmest. Six thousand years ago it became wetter, and just over 4,000 years ago there were significantly more gales and prolonged spells of heavy rainfall. Intriguingly, there was a 'Little Ice Age' between the sixteenth and eighteenth centuries. Perennial snowbeds, small ice patches and, arguably, small corrie glaciers formed in the Cairngorms, and there were some displacements of boulder lobes and terraces due to deep frost heave and thaws. Some of the travellers of the time mentioned snow lasting well into the summer on Ben Nevis in 1630, 1760 and 1787 (Bishop Pococke), and in the Cairngorms and Ben Wyvis, Thomas Pennant thought snow-lie was permanent in 1772. Two of our greatest meteorologists, Professors H. H. Lamb and G. Manley, added much to our knowledge of past climate change. Lamb suggested that the Cairn Gorm summit may have been permanently snow-covered between 1570 and 1770, whilst Manley summarised early recordings for Ben Nevis, and began a 'snow log' there in the Scottish Mountaineering Club hut in 1938 – inviting visitors to record their observations on snow cover.

Presently, the climate is warming, but still well within the temperate ranges that must have occurred 6,000-7,000 years ago. Climate change activated responses in vegetation. Woodland, with tall herbs and fern-rich understoreys, was at its maximum 7,000-8,000 years ago, shifting later and invariably to heaths and great blanket bogs under the deteriorating climate. Some bogs are over 9,000 years old, but the first major expanses formed more recently over the higher plateaux and in glen basins. What times these must have been, with trees and scrub marching and retreating – seeming to have scampered across the land at rates of half a kilometre a year or more.

Many puzzles remain. Why, for example, did Scots pine appear suddenly and then become extinct in much of western Scotland and Ireland 4,000 years ago? It seems that around just under 4,500 years ago the northern and western Highlands, and possibly the rest of the Highlands and Ireland, became much warmer for a period that lasted only 300-400 years. Then, Scots pine advanced rapidly around 80km north-westwards, and grew in places wholly unsuitable for it now. The next time you stand by a river in the far north-west look at its deep banks. Can you see a thin strip of tree stumps and roots plastered with fragments of pine bark? Four millennia ago something happened to this forest. Was it disease, or a great fire started by prehistoric settlers or by lightning? Or was it the overwhelming and stifling effects of peat accumulation as a result of climatic deterioration? Or was it linked with fallout from the volcanic eruption of Hekla-4 in Iceland, around

Looking south-west from Carn Dearg Meadhonach to Ben Nevis (opposite), with some near-permanent snowfields.

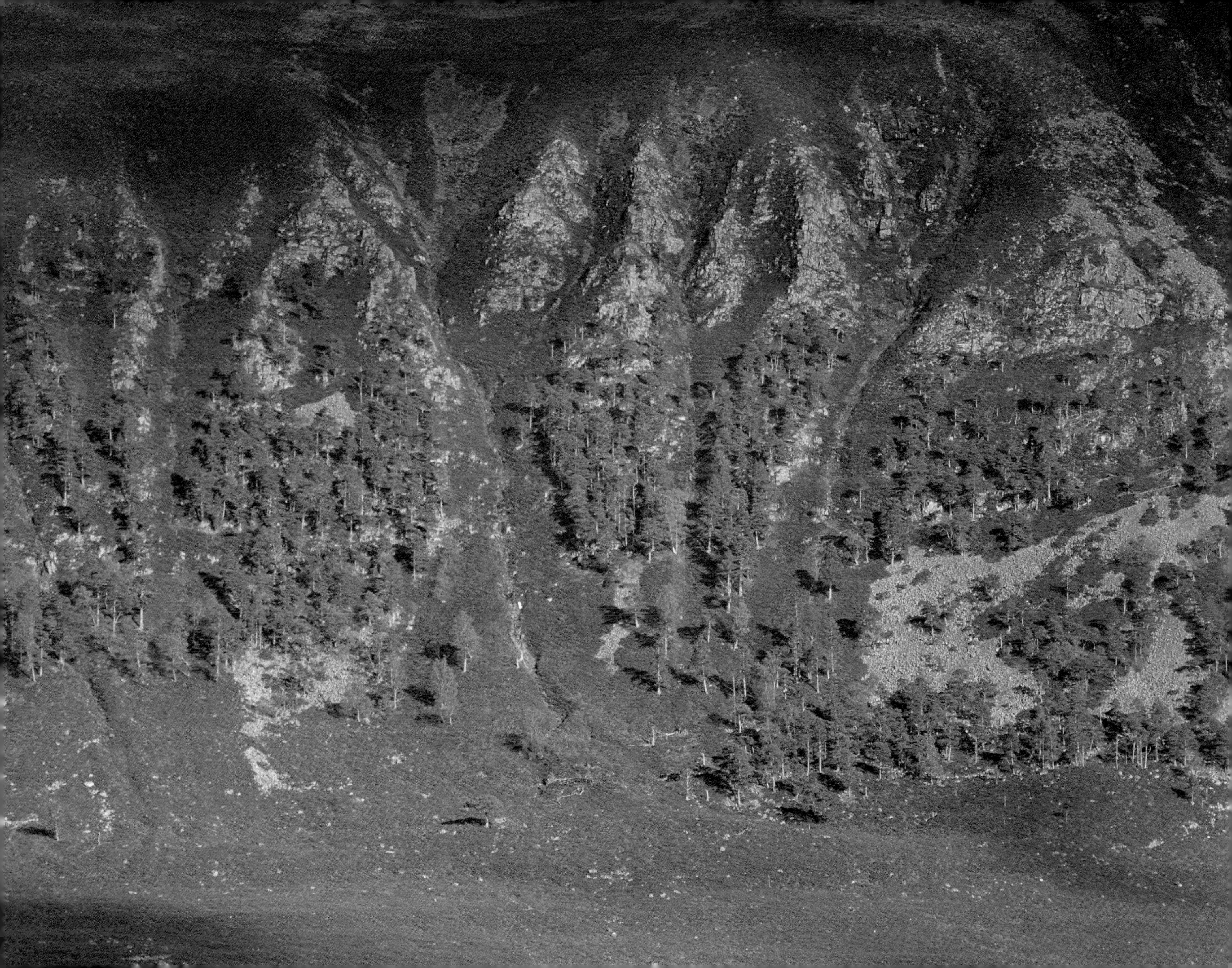

1,850 BC, and consequent catastrophic impacts on soil acidification, air quality and the great bogs? The pines died suddenly, but we don't know why.

Presently, only around 1% of the Great Wood of Caledon, as the Romans called it, remains. Most of this consists of remnant Scots pine clusters in Deeside and Speyside, and in the glens from Glen Moriston up to Glen Strathfarrar.

The Advent of Man and Forest Clearances

Now we can begin to distinguish between the natural phenomena and, for the first time, the mark of man. It is at Kinloch on Rum that we find some of the earliest evidence of hunter-gatherers in Scotland. From around 8,600 years ago there are Mesolithic, and Neolithic (just under 4,000 years old), remains of tools and charred vegetable food. Neolithic man first cleared major upland woods some 6,000 years ago. As time elapsed, increasingly large forests fell to cutting and, in the case of pine, to burning.

Woodland cover was probably at its maximum around 4,000 years ago when over 50% of Scotland was under trees. Intriguing patterns of vast forest clearance then emerge across the country, apparently for reasons still not clear to the experts. Here is the chronology summarised by Professor John Birks, with dates of the main onset of the most recent major clearances before present, BP, in brackets: Western Isles, Shetland and Caithness (4,500-4,200 BP), north-west Highlands and eastern Skye (3,900-3,700 BP), Sutherland and northern Skye (2,600-2,100 BP), south-west Scotland and southern Skye (1,700-1,400 BP) and, not so long ago, in the Grampians and Cairngorms (400-300 years BP).

Looking back over time we also see the onset of large-scale erosion, due to deforestation and the follow-up activities of burning and grazing, beginning some 1,700 years ago. Local atmospheric pollution was first evinced 2,000 years ago, but more widely from 700 years ago. Pollution has become serious only in the last 200 years, with major acidification of large lochs beginning some 120 years ago.

Remnants of the Caledonian forest on Creag Mhigeachaidh, Cairngorms (opposite) and in Glen Affric (above).

Present Day Conditions

Our climate is highly oceanic, influenced mainly by the Gulf Stream flowing north-eastwards from the Caribbean across the Atlantic. There is little seasonal variation in cloudiness, rainfall and temperature. Most of the rain, sleet and snow occurs between September and January, with December to February the coldest months and June to August the warmest. There is little sunshine, very high atmospheric humidity and strong winds. Similar conditions are highly unusual outwith the British Isles.

Another significant feature of our mountain climate is the steep gradients – both westwards and with rising altitude in high rainfall, more cloudiness, greater windspeed and coolness. The western Highlands can have double the number of wet days experienced in the east, and over 1°C separates the mean annual temperature of the southern Scottish uplands from the northern Highlands. The eastern Highlands are, therefore, more continental – milder in summer and colder in winter. Such differences may not seem important, but are indeed profound. The growing season for most vegetation persists as long as the average daily temperature exceeds 5°C (6°C for most grasses). A reduction of just 1°C from south to north shortens it by 6-10 weeks. The sight of newborn lambs in early May in Sutherland, almost two months later than their cousins in the Southern Uplands, confirms this picture of cooler conditions in the north.

Altitude has overriding effects on habitats, but there are variations across regions. As a rule temperature drops by 1°C with each 150m (492') climbed. Snowlie increases northwards, but is more intermittent in the milder west, and lasts 11-16 days longer for every 100m (328') gained in height. The summit of Ronas Hill (450m, 1475') on Shetland probably has a higher average windspeed than on Ben Nevis (1,343m, 4,408') – almost three times its altitude but some 300 miles south-west. Some exceptional gusts have been recorded, giving wind chill temperatures as low as -40°C!

Whilst slope, aspect and shelter affect ground level conditions for plants, at the regional level we see profoundly striking zones in vegetation. These descend downwards towards the Northern Isles and the north-west, giving impressions of the grand latitudinal belts of vegetation sweeping across northern Eurasia from temperate to polar regions. Towards the north and west are communities wholly characteristic of damp, windy, inhospitable climates – quite unlike the more eastern and southern British types with their continental affinities.

The High Mountain or 'Montane' Zone

Two major vegetation zones are recognised in the Scottish uplands. First, above the head dyke or upper reaches of enclosed farmland, there is the widespread **sub-montane zone** stretching up to the former tree-line. Most of this is moorland, bogland or grassland – derived from woodland but dominated now by dwarf-shrub heaths (mainly heather), grasses and sedges. This covers some 60% of Scotland and is the zone over which farmers, foresters, sporting estate managers and others struggle to make their living.

Above this, roughly upwards from 750m over most of Britain but lower to the north and west, is the **high mountain** or **montane zone**. The onset of this, marking the upper reaches of potential scrubby woodland, must be appreciated by all mountain walkers. We happen upon it suddenly as the dwarf-shrub heaths of heather and bilberry are no longer knee-deep but instead dwindle to just finger-high and prostrate. Just further up the slope are more mosses, lichens and cushion herbs, and with that bit more exposure there is that sudden sensation of openness.

We stride from one world to another. Moving with breathless ease, we leave places which have lost their woods and scrub, which have been burned and heavily grazed, and go on to near-natural places – some of which have barely changed in the space of 2,000 years. The soils are generally poor and infertile, and productivity is fairly low. But here we are on the least modified land in Britain. Only salt-marshes, sea cliffs

DRUMOCHTER (Ridge of Upper Ground) east of the Pass, scalloped by many shallow gullies and smooth corries, with a huge undulating high plateau of bog.

THE CAIRNGORM MOUNTAINS FROM THE NORTH

From Cairn Lochan (far left) west to Creag Dhubh above Gleann Einich (far right) there is woodland on the hill that has still to reach the former treeline. Scattered old pines in the foreground stand between planted forests. Here is a unique range of habitats –from woodland and heaths up to arctic-like fellfields, with breeding birds mirroring these transitions.

and ungrazed crags match the naturalness of this landscape, but the high mountain land is more extensive – covering around 3% of our British land surface, almost 7% of Scotland.

This special land begins at 700-800m (roughly 2,300'-2,600') in the Central Highlands, descending to 550m (1,805') in the North-West Highlands, 350m (1,149') by the north-west tip, and down to only 200-300m (656'-985') on Orkney and Shetland. Contrast this with tree-lines of 2,600m (8,534') in the Alps, 1,200m (3,939') in central Norway and below 500m (1,641') north of the Arctic Circle. Our mountains, with their distinctively low altitude tundra-like arctic-alpine heaths, are exceptional.

Habitats and Wildlife

Here, high up in the mountains, the so-called tree-lines have all but vanished, though there are remnants on cliff ledges inaccessible to sheep and deer. Whilst a mean summer temperature of less than 10°C during the two warmest months of the year seems to check tree growth and its upper limit, the knock-on suppressive effects of high windspeed have yet to be quantified accurately. A good wind-beaten example of Scots pine holds out at its upper brink on Creag Fhiaclach at 640m (2,100') in the western Cairngorms – claimed to be the only natural tree-line in the UK; Ben Loyal in Sutherland and some other northern hills also have close to the real vestiges. Although a taiga-type environment of Scots pine and predominant birch on better soils was prevalent in the north, further south there would have been cool, temperate mixed broad-leaved oak woods – called 'nemoral'.

The absence of extensive willow, scrubby birch and dwarf-birch at the scrub-line is curious. In western Norway there are vast sub-alpine scrub-heath plains that turn brilliant shades of red and purple in autumn. In Scotland all we have is the comparable understorey – depleted by the absence of diversity in stature. Will we ever really know what has been lost at the hands of nomadic high-altitude settlers with their 'slash and burn' practices and grazing animals (and perhaps much later, pollution)? Or is it just possible that Scotland and Norway have always been different in such respects, not least in the mountains with less fertile soils?

On the higher ground a fairly predictable pattern of vegetation emerges. Think of three prongs – exposure, elevation and waterlogging – and the pattern of vegetation falls into place. First there is heather, then higher where the climate is too rigorous for this, one finds bilberry – with much northern crowberry in parts. Above this, mat grass (sometimes with deer grass) occupies sheltered places where snow builds up, and finally late snow-patch vegetation forms where snow lingers late into summer. There are spanglings of mosses, liverworts, lichens and sparse grasses whose composition depends on the lateness of snowmelt. Over wetter ground the heather gives way to bilberry and hare's tail cotton grass, with prevalent crowberry, cowberry, northern bilberry, and bog mosses of course. Away from sheltered areas, exposed spurs and plateaux above the dwarf shrubs are dominated by carpets of woolly fringe moss (*Racomitrium lanuginosum*) with variable amounts of mountain sedge and least willow, and higher still there are loose, marbled patches of three-pointed rush and woolly fringe moss with a fragile lichen pile (mainly in the central and western Cairngorms).

The mossy carpet dominates the high foreground of many views from the high tops. Colours vary between all shades of gold, yellow and green depending on the light and recent showers of rain, and it is no wonder that many of these mossy, carpeted spurs are called A'Bhuidheanach or Meall Buidhe (the yellow place or hill). Some of our hills have their tops wholly dominated by this moss, such as Ben Wyvis, some of the Affric-Cannich Hills and the Drumochter tops (notably A'Mharconaich). This heath demands your special attention for it is the single most extensive near-natural plant community on land in the whole of the British Isles. In the far north and west there would be more carpet-like mossy heaths were it not for the rocky and more rugged nature of the summits, such as on Foinaven, Ben Hope and Ben Klibreck.

There are fascinating geomorphological processes afoot. Here are the moss-dominated hummocks and hollows, wrinkles and bumps, often arranged in laddered steps, which are the year-on-year product of freezing and thawing combined with the downwards or sideways movements of finer material. There are also stone nets and stripes, lobes and terraces, all bullworked by freeze-thaw processes and gravity. The montane plants *par excellence* are least willow and mountain sedge, whose presence earmarks this special, extreme place.

According to the latest classification of British vegetation we find 27 high mountain (i.e. montane) plant communities, most associated with either prolonged snow cover or exposure. Each community has its own assortment of species so that the sight of only two or three is sufficient to be diagnostic. The local occurrences of calcareous rocks and acid soils contribute in major ways to the diversity. In total, there are 121 montane flowering plants and ferns, and more than 200 mosses, liverworts, lichens and fungi. One has to be regularly amongst the corries, boulder fields and scree slopes, however, to notch up close to the full tick list of these plants.

The distribution of this mountain vegetation does not wholly respect the geological boundaries mentioned earlier. Instead, the vegetation 'bio-regions' are demarcated first in an east-westerly direction by the amount of coolness, wetness and windiness, and then by the amount of high and extensive terrain. There are also north-south divides but, perhaps surprisingly, it is the impact of man rather than the northerly deterioration in climate that dictates these. But we dwell on this later on.

Interacting with their Scottish montane habitats are the animals – including 23 species of breeding birds, 12 mammals and probably 2,000-3,000 of the large invertebrates – chiefly insects and spiders (including at least 100 confined to high ground). The uplands as a whole contain 71 breeding birds; mountains as such are not their most popular haunt. Only three specialists typically belong to montane areas – resident ptarmigan, migratory dotterel and snow bunting – and

FROST-HEAVE HUMMOCKS, DRUMOCHTER

These hummocks dominated by woolly fringe moss (*Racomitrium lanuginosum*) form through the cyclical actions of freezing and thawing.

Well above the former tree-line there are local areas where soil creeps downwards under gravity and frost action (solifluction). Crumples form, and some may still be active – each year adding another millimetre or so to the hummocks. These and other such features are 'periglacial' – characteristic of cold climates. Some of these may have been active for several thousand years.

THE DOTTEREL (*Charadrius morinellus*)

This little gem is a male, and he alone usually cares for the clutch of three eggs and chicks. Dotterel are beautiful, colourful and exciting birds. The Gaelic name is *Amadan Mointeach*, 'mossfool', on account of the remarkable tameness of the male. He can show great tenacity in returning to the nest within a few metres of the observer.

Their favourite nesting habitat is hummocky, montane woolly fringe moss, with the nest scoop close to the top of the mound. Some individuals have bred in both Scotland and Norway – just occasionally in the same year.

studies of these have given some extraordinary insights into the natural processes of change.

The dotterel is truly fascinating. Its lifestyle was likened by the late Desmond Nethersole-Thompson, in his classic monograph (1973), to that under a petticoat government. This amazing bird breeds on the tops where the male, usually alone, cares for eggs and chicks whilst the more striking female can mate with several males. Recent work has shown the dotterel population to number some 860 'pairs', with much movement by individuals between Norwegian and Scottish Highland breeding grounds. There are substantial differences between some tops in the productivity of populations – and some rely on recruits from others to maintain their numbers. A beautiful bird, it has earned the nickname 'mossfool' on account of its tameness by the nest. Such is the appeal of the bird's colourful antics that *The Scotsman* ran a full-page advert for it on 27 July 1994 with the eyecatcher: 'Promiscuous female leaves five lovers and fifteen offspring for wild sex in Scandinavia', before going on to mention an account of the above research work that it had covered on the previous day.

The golden eagle is perhaps the icon of the Scottish mountains. More than any other animal, this bird typifies the grandeur, majesty and mystery of our wild land. During 1982-3 and 1992 comprehensive surveys were made of virtually all eagle home ranges in Scotland. Numbers occupied during these two periods have changed little (491 compared with 511) with some 420 ranges having pairs. In 1992, 182 pairs reared 210 flying young, with the eastern Highlands having more successful pairs than the Western Isles. The highest breeding densities of birds are found in the Outer and Inner Hebrides and the western Highlands where population density seems to be highest where the abundance of carrion, principally dead sheep and red deer, is greatest. Even over the last 10 years there have been some marked increases and decreases in numbers of breeding pairs across different parts of Scotland, apparently because of changes in breeding success. But what is accounting for these changes remains to be shown.

THE PTARMIGAN (*Lagopus mutus*)

This hardy bird is virtually confined to the montane zone – breeding above 750m in the central Cairngorms, but down to around 550m in the western Highlands and even to 300m in the far north-west. It is strongly territorial, though the birds form packs in winter when they can move downhill well below their normal habitat. The ptarmigan is probably a relict species from the Ice Age more than 10,000 years ago, when the breeding range would have been much more extensive.

Ptarmigan feed on blaeberry throughout the year, with tiny fresh shoots being vital for hens during egg laying.

The ptarmigan is one of the toughest birds on land – anywhere – able to withstand exceptionally cold climates. It feeds largely on dwarf shrubs, particularly the blaeberry. Breeding ptarmigan have gone from mountains south of the Highlands, and this has been linked with the eradication of montane dwarf shrubs under heavy sheep-grazing pressure. More recently, there have been declines in the South-West Highlands, and this may be linked with more predation, habitat deterioration or even changes in climate.

A Diverse Land

It is the variation in character of Scottish mountains that is so eye-catching. Towards the west the mountain massifs are rugged and steep – the result of heavy glaciation. The Cheviots are much more gently contoured, and the Grampian hills in the east have broad sweeping plateaux. The most massive mountains are clustered in the central Highlands, though one can be deceived to the contrary wandering from Knoydart through Glen Shiel and then over to Glen Affric.

Wildlife varies also. The wealth of upland birds is greatest in the central Highlands – and on the flows and maritime heaths of the north and east where more arctic birds add to the tally. The western craggy hulks and peninsulas are not so bountiful – though of course there are golden eagles and ptarmigan breeding higher up – with the central and eastern moors, bogs and smoother tops having more birds such as dotterel, golden plover and dunlin.

The plants are quite another matter. The richer, more basic (as opposed to acid) rocks are very localised in Scotland, but where these are found there is a wonderfully luxuriant flora. The Breadalbane mountains, from Ben Lawers to Ben Lui, are the best, with Ben Lawers special for alpine plants, having rich rocks right up to its summit. Other important areas are Caenlochan, Glen Doll, Corrie Fee and Corrie Kanders in Angus and Aberdeenshire; Beinn Dearg and Seana Braigh in Ross-shire – the most northerly of the truly high mountains in Scotland with outposts of some of our arctic-alpine rarities – and local parts of the North-West Highlands (such as Inchnadamph) and of the Southern Uplands, notably the Moffat Hills. The Cairngorms area is a world apart from the rest. The great stature of this massif, with its cold climate and high elevation of corries and gullies, supports a bewildering mixture and array of plants. There are many calcifuges that love acid rocks (for the prevailing bedrock is granite), calcicoles (that need basic rock) on the schists, as well as the hardy specialists of narrow zones of late snowlie and harsh, exposed fellfields.

Do not be deceived by the typical vegetation cover on the hill for this is dominated mainly by heaths, grasses and sedges with a fairly low richness of species. But on the ledges and crevices of exposed crags and gullies, and in boulder fields and scree slopes, there are scores of flowering plants not found at lower elevation but which thrive here in the virtual absence of grazing and competition. Some delightful names reflect the demeanour of these plants: blue sow-thistle, alpine speedwell, starry saxifrage and alpine hawkweed. But what lush hanging gardens there are on some of the cliffs. If you are lucky you will see several of the mountain willows and you should see roseroot, wood crane's-bill, stone bramble, red campion, alpine saw-wort and mountain sorrel. If you venture to the richest areas you should see the famous rarities like alpine milk-vetch, snow gentian, mountain bladder-fern, drooping saxifrage and even alpine forget-me-not. But then you may be lucky enough to come across some of these outwith Ben Lawers or Caenlochan-Clova, on other mountains where they have been discovered more recently.

The hillwalker or mountaineer should take interest in the vegetation on the high tops and note its profound contrasts. Just look at the summit heaths and see how these tend to be lichen-infested towards the east and in parts of the central Highlands, but moss-dominated towards the west and north. These are the natural indicators of the drier, colder more continental conditions of the east compared with the cloud-sodden, wet and windy tops of the west. The mosaics of heather, deer sedge/grass, purple moor grass and bog myrtle towards the west, but of somewhat drier heather moors with bilberry and bog cottons further east, attest wonderfully to the east-west differences in climatic influences on the lower slopes of the hills.

Sample these and other such clines by going east over Beinn Eighe, Fionn Bheinn, some of the Fannichs and then to Ben Wyvis; or go from Foinaven to Ben Hope, then to Ben Loyal and Ben Klibreck and finally to the dainty duo of Morven and Scaraben. Too far north? Well, take the train to Glenfinnan, then to Tulloch at Glen Spean and finally travel on to Dalwhinnie. Climb the nearest Munros to each. Stand high, east of Drumochter, perhaps on Carn na Caim, and see the big Bens in the west sunk deep in mist and cloud. To the north-east the Cairngorms are dry – well perhaps drier. But under you there is woolly fringe moss and lichen, and to the west more moss and damp wet heaths. Students of nature could do little better than come here to appreciate the living mantle of our mountains.

Even on a single hill we see some of these climate-imposed differences. Those related to elevation have already been noted, but what of those experienced in the traverse? The north-west slopes (clockwise round to east facing) get the least direct sun and have more liverworts (small bryophytes which, unlike related mosses, look rather seaweed-like), many of which thrive on cool, damp shaded areas. The western slopes have more woolly fringe moss in carpet-like heather whilst on the east there are more lichens in communities of stunted heather and bilberry. Facing south the montane zone is much less extensive. Here, trees formerly grew higher up, and there are more grasses and sedges. The pattern of snowlie varies considerably also, as experienced winter mountaineers will confirm, and the largest snowfields persist for longest on north-eastern slopes. As ever, such natural patterns are never simple, and there are countless exceptions to even the simplest of rules. Even the hills themselves exert effects of shelter and shading with consequences for some of their neighbours.

The character and diversity of the land is the sum product of the rocks, soils, habitats and wildlife, but also of the impacts of climate, man and his beasts. Behold this beauty on each hill and in every district

– the arrangement of communities like that of notes in a tune.

Fraser Darling captured perfectly the spirit of nature in the mountains when he wrote:

The deep and precipitous corries and the spiry summits may cause awe, but the high grasslands on a summer day have an idyllic quality. They are remote and quiet. They are green and kind to the eye. They are ease to the feet. The flowers have great variety and a new beauty, and the very pebbles among which they grow have a sparkle and show of colour. To climb to one of these alps of grass and descend again in a few hours is not enough. Take a little tent and remain in the quietness for a few days. It is magnificent to rise in the morning in such a place. The only sounds breaking the silence, if you get the best of the early July weather, will be the grackle of the ptarmigan, the flute-like pipe of the ring ouzel, and perhaps the plaint of a golden plover or a dotterel. See how the deer, now bright-red-coated, lie at ease in the alpine grassland. Listen, if you have stalked near enough, to the sweet talkings of the calves who are like happy children. Of your charity disturb them not in their Arcadia.

F. Fraser Darling, *Natural Hisory in the Highlands and Islands*, 1947

Affinities With Other Places

Internationally, the Scottish mountains are significant. Their habitats represent southern and oceanic outliers of arctic-alpine fellfield and arctic tundra. The highest places, with their stony summit plateaux and snowbeds are fragmentary neighbours of south-west Norway (moving northwards from, for example, the Hardanger) and of lands as far apart as the Canadian arctic, Greenland and the Gory Byrranga in northern Russia. There are some communities unique or distinctive in Scotland, and others more widespread here than elsewhere globally. The montane heathery heaths are scarce outside Scotland. Our fern, lichen and moss-dominated vegetation is staggeringly rich. Yet our upland higher plant flora is poor compared with the continent.

Some plants assemble with remarkable allies and take on an appearance not seen elsewhere. The range of plants, drawn from boreal, arctic, temperate, atlantic, alpine and continental regions is unique. On lower ground, the long history of land management is not known elsewhere. The mixture of birds is highly unusual, with tiny fringe populations of some arctic birds, major outliers of others as well as of more temperate species, and globally high densities of ptarmigan and dotterel, and of red grouse, golden eagle, golden plover, peregrine and raven breeding lower down.

There are endless surprises in the mountains, and travels abroad merely confirm the great beauty and diversity of our gaunt land. The resemblance to western and southern Norway is certainly striking. But there is a harshness to our land that forces us to look here for features utterly absent. I have gone on successive days to Ben Macdui (1,309m) from the Hardanger Vidda (1,691m) – between Bergen and Oslo – and searched in vain for glaciers. I have taken for granted the vast scrubby mosaics of 'dwarf' birch and willow scrub dwindling naturally into stunted high mountain heaths in the Dovrefjell, south of Trondheim, and glanced only a cursory eye over the richest mountain flora in the whole of northern Europe there. Yet on returning I was disappointed at the relatively impoverished flora and stature of our plants. Even in the Austrian Tirol I readily took to the large summer snow-fields and high forests, yet on coming home noticed immediately, in Knoydart as it happened, the total absence of high woodland and little more than small patches of snow.

Many other instances of this nature come to mind, yet always our wild places seem more charming. It is a matter of scale, for here we have access to many ecosystems and landscapes that occur elsewhere more grandly yet much further apart. This seems the greatest virtue. The sweeping and haunting flow country of the north – so tangibly similar to the open, low Arctic wet tundra – is but a few hours drive from the pine forest of Abernethy and the barren fellfield of Cairn Gorm. And later we can travel on to Loch Hourn in the west and be in a Norwegian fjord-like sea loch by nightfall. But to make such journeys abroad within the confines of a region, even a country, is less feasible in a day.

LOCH NEVIS – A fjordic sealoch, with Eigg in the distance.

THE QUIRAING, North Trotternish, Isle of Skye – labyrinths of basalt lavas that have collapsed over weaker, underlying sedimentary rocks.

Of all natural elements, it is possibly the oceanic climate that inflicts such variability on the land. Comparable mountain areas abroad have more rainfall and higher temperatures (New Zealand and Southern Oceanic uplands), much lower winter temperatures (north-east Asian mountains of northern Japan and Kamchatka), lower windspeeds with cooler temperatures (Patagonia) and much more seasonal variation in temperature, more akin to continental climates (parts of the Uralskiy Khhrebet running north in central Russia, and even the coastal mountains along eastern Canada). The maritime western mountains of Canada and the Alaska range are not so different in climate but are much more massive in stature.

For British mountains, the nearest affinities are with Ireland (which is warmer), south-western Norway (with more northerly winds and less equable temperatures) and to some extent with the Faroe Islands (rather like the Trotternish peninsula on Skye, with a cooler climate than here).

It is to Norway, however, that we should look for similarities. Here, in the oceanic mountains around the forbidding Sognefjord, is a climate and vegetation so alike what is and was ours. Flying east towards Bergen, 60 miles to the south, we are struck first by the huge coverage of pine, birch and spruce forest on small islands and mainland alike with only small clearings for sæters (hill farms). On the surrounding mountains, richly wooded ramparts rise out of the sea giving up juniper, dwarf birch and willow scrub, then comparably bare fellfields and immense snowfields higher still. Everywhere, it seems, there are trees – even on the rockiest of islets and craggiest of cliffs. Is this as Scotland was some 5,000-8,000 years ago? Yes, probably, but by the period of Viking invasions a good deal of our woodland had gone.

Cultural and socio-economic contrasts are equally stark. In Norway, with just over 4 million people and a quarter of these in rural parts, there is less dependency on arable farmland (2% of land) but more on forest and woodland (27% of land). The valleys seem that bit more productive and the farms are small and owned individually, though the mountain grazings are shared. There is close integration with forestry and a pleasing jumble of small fields, productive and natural forests and farm buildings nestling between the sea and mountain hulks. Compare this with western Scotland – empty glens with abandoned crofts, huge blocks of conifer plantations and only small remnants of woodland pointing the way ahead. Many of the farms that stand out on the hill are tied to large estates whose major objective may be the sport-related pursuit of red deer or grouse. There are many more sheep and deer than the hill can sustain for itself, and ugly pocks and scars, even whole denuded hill slopes, mark the remains of untended fires.

Just Being There!

For thousands of mountaineers, hillwalkers, and sightseers the details of environmental aspects – past and present – may have mattered little. Instead, it is simply being there that is important, and in some ways the plethora of knowledge spoils our mountain deism. We experience cloud-dripping, wind beaten and bleak days on the hill, but also special times with tingling mixtures of deep veneration, elation and inspiration.

I am moved by the beauty and nature of these places, and by the powerful union of light, land and life. I thrill at the prospect of a new top. The return to a familiar place is eagerly awaited; the birds and plants, the views and impressions, that peculiarly intoxicating excitement of reaching the summit – all contribute to milestone experiences and to the continuation of life at its best. Millions of words have been written on these things, and to each of us their use and moods have singularly different meanings.

We are entering a period of stark change, however, so profound that our mountains will never again be as they were to earlier generations. The mountains are under more pressure now than ever before, from people, and from sheep, deer, conifer trees, skiing developments, pollution and even climate change. The problems are not insurmountable – some should be readily resolved. The most extraordinary new statistic, however, is simply this: the chance of spending a day on the hill alone is close to zero. In just 30 years there has been something like a ten-fold rise in the number of hillwalkers (the figure has at least doubled during the 1980s). Whilst the cultural and social fabric of wild places continues to disintegrate, and livelihoods in crofting, farming, fishing and traditional light industries teeter nervously, swelling ranks of people converge on the hills for their leisure.

There is a growing zest for health and fitness, new personal challenges (preferably physical) and for escapism. The mountains are there to meet this need, and prolific sales of slick mountain books attest to this. The growing fad for guides is in some ways depressing, meeting a need in people to be led; but the upsurge in concern for mountain areas is a consolation. The actual number of visitors is staggering. In 1991, Scotland attracted just under 10 million tourists (84% from the UK), and Scottish people alone made 85 million day trips to the countryside (compared with around 25 million in 1973). As many as a quarter of these visitors probably came into contact with mountain areas. High tops, such as Ben Nevis and Cairn Gorm, may have up to 1,000 visitors on a fine day. Is it any wonder that over 80% of overseas visitors, surveyed recently by the Scottish Tourist Board, put scenery at the top of their list of what attracted them to Scotland? And the enterprise is remarkable, with the entire Scottish tourist industry generating some £2.5 billion and serving over 180,000 jobs.

The Munros and Allies of Folly

Some argue that the brigands who seek their 'Munro scalps' scarcely deserve mention. Why set as your personal Everest a mountain at least 3,000 feet (or a prosaic 914 metres) high? With their high-tech clothing, heads to the ground and scant care for the mountain mood, these 'baggers' haul their carcasses to the top intent merely on notching a point. To be fair, neither the baronet knight Hugh Thomas Munro of Lindertis, who in September 1891 first published his tables of 3,000' mountains in Scotland, nor the Scottish Mountaineering Club, ever intended such an attitude.

For the record, the Scottish Mountaineering Club presently recognises 277 Munro mountains and 517 tops in Scotland. There is debate about what separates one mountain summit or peak, as opposed to several tops, from another. Most of the cognoscenti agree that there should be a 100 foot drop between tops, giving a widely accepted 281 peaks plus 287 tops over 3,000'. England has four such peaks and three tops, Wales has eight peaks and six tops, and Ireland has seven peaks and six tops.

The Corbetts, named after John Rooke Corbett, refer to hills between 2,500' (762m) and 3,000' with a drop of at least 500' (152.4m) between them, of which there are 221. There are 87 Donalds, named after Percy Donald, covering every 2,000'-2,500' hill in the Scottish lowlands. And there are Grahams, more than 250 of them, scaling 2,000'-2,500' in the Scottish Highlands and Islands. Named after Fiona Torbet (née Graham) the listing of these began in a hospital bed. *The Scotsman* of 14 November 1992 ran an editorial poking just a little fun at these terms under the banner 'Heights of folly'. Does such categorisation of these mountains demean their individuality and character?

Here we are concerned mainly with high mountain areas. These rise above roughly 3,000', but many are as low as 2,300' – just over 700m. The variability of these places renders it pointless to apply maverick terms to the height of a mountain. Rather, we hope to display the diversity of the land and its nature, building on our knowledge of gestations, processes and the elements.

GLENCOE – Bold, rugged, revered and poignantly special.

MAN AND LAND-USE

Scotland is nothing without its people. But the people of Scotland are nothing without Scotland – and our aim must be to ensure that this Scotland of ours continues to be worth living in.
Magnus Magnusson, *The Nature of Scotland*, 1991

The end of the seventeenth century heralded an important era embracing a unique interplay between man, politics and what is now our natural heritage. The population of Scotland numbered approximately one million people with over 80% of them subsisting on the land. There was great starvation in the wake of persistent crop failures and many communities were reduced by a quarter.

Following the '45 Jacobite Rebellion there were dramatic changes to the management of land. Enormous areas came under the ownership of the 'Great Landlords' and there was a general expansion of large estates. Drainage, liming, construction of enclosures and crop rotations all became established practices, though these took some 80 years to reach the remoter upland areas. The mixed traditional economy dependent on cattle, sheep, goats and some arable gave way through wholescale clearances of people to sheep. The private estate blossomed as the 1800s brought abject misery and unrest amongst much of the rural populance of the Highlands.

Two striking changes then set the scene for the modern-day uplands. Firstly, during the 1830s and 1840s the 'clearances' reached their awful pitch and, for the first time, the urban populations in Scotland outnumbered those in rural areas. Secondly, during the 1860s and early 1870s, in particular, the landowners reaped their greatest profits and invested much capital in shooting lodges, Victorian mansions, estate buildings and, most bizarrely, in the patchwork burning of heather moorland for red grouse, and at a grander and more slapdash scale, for red deer. The uplands of this time took on an altogether more open and modified appearance – the butt end of two hundred years of 'cultural' landscape change.

Deer, Grouse and Sheep

A visitor coming to the Scottish mountains for the first time is struck by the peculiar arrangement of grouse moor, deer-forest and sheep-walk – all a product of the recent changes mentioned above. It was F. Fraser Darling and J. Morton Boyd, two pioneer naturalist-ecologists, who first formalised descriptions of these habitats in their classic book *The Highlands and Islands* (1964). As they say about deer-forest:

> *The fact of two and a half million acres of deer forest in the Highlands has been a matter for congratulation or for execration, dependent on whether the comments come from a sportsman, a naturalist, a sheep farmer or crofter or a member of a political party opposed to the existence of what is considered an anomaly in modern times.*

Whilst sheep-walk today takes in mainly the Cheviots and Southern Uplands, deer-forest covers the western Highlands (south to north) and much of the central Highlands. Grouse moor is the major land-use in the eastern Highlands and lower upland reaches of the central Highlands. There is much overlap across regions, notably between sheep-walk and grouse moor, and more locally between sheep-walk and deer-forest. Overall, agriculture now tends to lead as the main land-use with some 80% of the land in agricultural production.

Most of the deer-forests had come about by the mid 1800s, though some had been established as early as 1770 (notably in Aberdeenshire). Some of these forests became more intensively managed as sheep-farming declined following poor sheep sales. Contemporary deer-forest covers just under 20% of Scotland.

The heavy imprints of man – muirburn, grazing sheep and some forestry. Looking towards Glen Truim, Badenoch (opposite).

But hunts for deer began much earlier, and the records show that Malcolm III of Canmore regularly pursued deer in Monar in the late eleventh century. Indeed, some of the early royal hunts were expensive affairs, with 300 men a day involved in Atholl and Mar Estate hunts. Ironically, the deer-forests are now largely treeless, with some of their original woodland destroyed by the end of the eighteenth century. Indeed, the red deer is a rapacious suppressor of woodland regeneration, taking seedlings and barking saplings before the trees can develop beyond the reaches of their foe. The moribund remnants of the central Highland Great Caledonian pinewood, first recorded by Pliny, is a particularly glum sight. Here a once great forest has been humbled by the extinction of progeny, yet has obvious promise where there is spectacular regeneration in fenced-off areas without deer.

Red deer in Scotland live at the edge of their world range and, by dint of the harsh and infertile nature of their habitat, attain a smaller size than elsewhere in Europe. Their population has more than doubled to almost 350,000 in the past 30 years. The deer 'problem' has vexed many governments (there have been seven government-appointed enquiries between 1872 and 1954!), not least because of conflicts with agriculture and forestry as well as because of aspects of cruelty and control. Attention has recently turned to the deterioration of the land, its natural habitats and wildlife. The government is looking at means of checking deer numbers in relation to what the land can sustain – an unenviable challenge. It does seem, however, that one key to the control of deer in harmony with their habitat lies with culling large numbers of hinds, rather than stags, for these tend to occupy the richer feeding areas, compelling stags to feed on the more sensitive heathery stands.

Most of the red deer range is above 2,000 feet (609m) so it is in winter, when shelter is needed, that the woods and surrounding moorland patches are particularly hard hit by grazing. However, the spectacle of the rut in October, as stags defend their harems, is truly thrilling. The great deer-forests of Mar, Lochnagar, Rothiemurchus and those scattered north and west of the Great Glen, and on richer hills such as Drumochter and Caenlochan, come alive in autumn and offer some memorable theatre. Indeed, such places offer some of the wildest elements of our mountain wildlife. It is little wonder that the nature of deer-forest ownership and management is so robustly debated.

The other upland sporting enterprise, grouse shooting, occupies a somewhat different niche. The grouse moor arose slightly earlier than open deer-forest, with large-scale shooting taking off in the early nineteenth century, reaching a peak towards the latter half of that century, which was then maintained through to the mid-1930s. Heather, the main food of red grouse, is burned regularly and in strips to provide ideal mixtures of young plants for food and older stands for shelter and nesting. The ensuing densities of red grouse can be phenomenal, and numbers shot defy belief. The record 'bag' for Scotland stands at 2,523 birds killed by eight guns on 30 August 1891 at Roan Fell in the Southern Uplands – another 1,266 birds were shot there eight days later.

Just over 250,000 grouse are now shot annually in Scotland, the majority coming from the 300 grouse moor estates occupying almost 14,000 square kilometres (almost three times the size of Sutherland). To cover its costs an estate should, on average, produce for each square kilometre approximately 60 grouse and a harvest of 27 birds. The sport generates a total revenue of £5.3 million and creates the equivalent of 1,700 full-time jobs. Yet many moors run at a loss, with estate running costs coming from other sources of income. The future of grouse moors in Scotland remains uncertain, with continuing debate about the effects of predation by both foxes and raptors, parasites, louping-ill and moorland habitat loss. The wine-red moors of the central and eastern Highlands provide especially serene vistas in August, so much so that these are accepted as part of our native and wild romantic landscape.

There are around 2.4 million sheep in the uplands of Scotland, and on these, communities of crofters and farmers are dependent. Most of the hills have grazing sheep, and one of the most intriguing aspects to this is the extent to which sheep have caused the hill to deteriorate

RED DEER (*Cervus elaphus*)

Red deer are a quintessential part of the mountains, and deer estate management dominates much of the Highlands.

The current population of just under 300,000 is widely regarded as too high. The grazing and browsing effects of deer on woodland and hill vegetation continue to vex many conservationists.

The provision of food for deer in winter has probably reduced their chances of death and so has contributed to increasing numbers.

Red deer are rarely in the mountains above 3,000' during autumn through to spring, but from May onwards they move higher up – the stags spending more time in the glen bottoms whilst the hinds are on the more fertile sub-alpine grasslands. However, they will often go lower down at night to feed, when in the cooler conditions biting flies are less active.

We still know little about the ranging behaviour of deer. Some observers have seen huge herds of between 1,800 and 2,400 animals moving onto the high plateaux of the western Cairngorms after dusk, offering a unique spectacle of noise, movement and the reek of disturbed peat.

There are over 50 Deer Management Groups in Scotland, and these seem to offer the best prospects for strategic red deer culls. Increasingly, estates will need to work together to control and manage deer – which can range over several estates in any one year.

GLEN LYON – Looking east from Balnahanaid.

ecologically. In the latter part of the nineteenth century there was talk of a downturn in the quality and productivity of hill grazings, mainly in the northern Highlands. Sandy Mather, a geographer at Aberdeen University, made a valuable study of this and found, curiously, a rise in lambing performance in the east, but a decline in the west over the past 100 years. Such trends have been symptomatic of what is termed the 'wet desert' effect in the western Highlands, where soil fertility, game bags, the abundance of wildlife and agricultural production all seem to have declined. There is no simple answer, but there does seem to have been more soil erosion recently, and this may well be linked with more intense burning and stocking rates than the land can sustain in the west.

What is clear, however, but only now coming to be widely accepted, is that swathes of the high ground have become grassier and duller floristically under prolonged grazing by sheep. Just look out for the tell-tale fence-lines or dyke-lines, where heather, other dwarf shrubs and even scrubby woodland are better formed and intact on one side compared with the other. The same can be seen on fenced-off or inaccessible slopes and crags, with the diversity of plant life greater out of reach of sheep. It is true that deer also account for some of these contrasts, but such examples extend far outwith their core range, from the copious evidence of sheep grazing impacts in the Southern Uplands, all the way north to Orkney and Shetland. Some of the most striking examples occur between road and fence where, over just a few metres, heather can grow in the absence of sheep – some of the best lessons here being along the Carter Bar linking Scotland and England, and along the A9 north of Dalwhinnie!

Perhaps during the Bronze Age period (1,850-1,200 years BC) in the North-West Highlands but much later into Medieval (eleventh to sixteenth centuries) and even the Tudor and Stuart (sixteenth to seventeenth centuries) periods in much of the rest of upland Scotland, dwarf shrub heaths covered the lower deforested hills. Repeated burning would have wiped out the woody species, such as heather, and grazing pressures would have added to the steady further conversion to grasses and even to bracken. Then, as seen now, the mountain dwarf shrubs came to be quite restricted, in many parts to rocky slopes or peaty areas. Soil erosion must date back far in some parts, with screes on steep slopes often resulting from heavy grazing and burning.

The most fertile uplands seem to have suffered the heaviest grazing pressure, so it is not surprising that on the Breadalbanes much heathery vegetation has been lost from early times. It is difficult to be precise about the nature of habitat loss to grazing sheep, not least because the farmers' use of in-bye land (lying between the upper reaches of arable land and the head-dyke), application of fertilisers and use of winter food supplements all influence the impact on heather. But there is a simple rule: where sheep remove around 40% or less of the season's growth of heather it will persist; where they remove more than this – up to around 80% of the fresh growth – it will hold out, but only partly; and where more than 80% is taken the heather will not regenerate and will, in time, be lost. It is in autumn and winter that heather is grazed most intensively by sheep (for it is the only major evergreen available) and where supplementary food blocks lie on the hill there may, in time, be another line of retreating heather where sheep have grazed too heavily whilst concentrating there to feed.

The other simple rule, that holds for the Southern Uplands, is that where sheep graze at less than two ewes to the hectare, heather moorland will be in good condition, where there are two to four ewes the heather will be poor or even suppressed, and where there are more than four ewes to the hectare the heather may well be absent. Towards the north and west, and in the higher districts, much lower densities of sheep account for comparable damage to heather. So often one views the hill, with its mosaic of scrub, heather and grassland, without appreciating just what has been lost and gained – and why.

Heather moorland covers almost 25% of Scotland but is contracting fast under forestry and under grazing sheep. The main losses started 200 years ago where there were high concentrations of sheep on the open hill, but in the North-West Highlands moorland losses may have begun only at the turn of the nineteenth century. The recent losses of heather amount to approximately a quarter of the extent present in the mid 1940s (something like the full area of Lothian Region has therefore vanished), with a further 30-40% of the remaining moor set to dwindle away within the next 20 years. The pattern of loss on the ground is often very similar: the heather gets so heavily grazed that it becomes topiary or drumstick in appearance, then bilberry appears briefly before grasses come in as the heather cover drops to under a half of the area, and later still the heather becomes scarce as the purple moor grass and mat grass takes hold and spreads. With the demise of these heaths, under present-day numbers of sheep, will pass the myriad of mosaics of different aged and sized habitats abounding in a rich wealth of birds, invertebrates and plants – making up what should be a uniquely sustainable managed landscape.

The impact of grazing sheep, and deer also, on other upland habitats is much harder to assess. Many of the mountain 'alpine' grasslands have arisen from the combined effects of soil acidity, prolonged wetness and long-standing grazing by sheep. Even on the highest tops, where sheep eke out a living for only a few months in spring and summer, there is evidence of fragmentation and more direct damage to fragile mossy and lichen-dominated heaths. Whether this diminution is occurring more rapidly than on the moorlands below remains to be quantified. Certainly, south of the Scottish Highlands there are no summit heaths that have escaped the ravages of sheep, but then there are high mountains in Ross-shire and Sutherland with superb summit fellfields that have changed little this century.

Forestry

The large-scale planting of conifers has not affected the landscape of the high mountains, though there are now few hills without partially-wooded lower flanks. Only some 14% of Scotland (10% of Britain) is now forested. Only three of the developed countries in the world have less of their land devoted to forestry – Ireland, the Netherlands and Australia – adding much of the impetus to re-afforest Scotland. We have already dwelt on the loss of natural woodland, and the desire for reparation and restitution is understandable. But the tide of public opinion seems to have shifted against large-scale conifer plantations, favouring instead the expansion of existing remnants of mixed and broad-leaved woods.

A desire for many ecologists and foresters is the re-creation of huge forests across the country, with the full range of wildlife variation that would have been present, east to west and from the low ground to the upper reaches. Moving down from the north there should be mixtures of scrub and open boggy heaths, then birchwoods, with hazel and scattered oak, then (into Ross-shire and south throughout the Highlands) great pinewoods with birch, and, in the south, mixed deciduous woods predominantly with oak and hazel. If you have wandered through Rothiemurchus Forest, Abernethy or the Quoich in Deeside *en route* to the Cairngorms' tops you will understand this dream. But the modern conifer blocks of spruce, larch and lodgepole pine that blight so many landscapes, hamper access and, in places, facilitate the acidification of streams and lochs, are not part of this vision.

The future balance between forested and open landscapes will be hotly debated. Since 1924 over one million hectares of the uplands have been afforested. Now further upland afforestation in Britain is virtually confined to Scotland where Regional Forest Strategies indicate areas as desirable for forestry or otherwise. Many upland conservationists still regard afforestation with the greatest concern and point to post-war losses of open habitat, rare plants and breeding birds. One has only to spend time in the hills of Galloway or Argyll, or to look out over the once continuously open great peatland flows of Caithness and Sutherland, to see their point.

Pollution

As we look out across the Grampians to Ben Nevis and its legions there is a slight haziness to the view. Way back in time this would have been

STRATH OSSIAN, at the southern end of Loch Laggan, with a herd of red deer, a wedge of forestry and massive hill country in the distance.

much worse. Think of the volcanoes belching and wheezing and others with leaking cracks and fissures. The Central Belt must have reeked, with Arthur's Seat and the Ochil Hills presiding over pong-dripping rainforests some 300 million years ago! It is hard to picture comparable volcanic activity on Skye, Islay, Mull and Ardnamurchan. In more recent times the Lakigigar eruption in Iceland in AD 1783-1784, which produced the world's greatest lava flow, was felt in Caithness where 1783 was referred to as 'the year of the ashie'. Now the world has to cope with the after-effects of pollution and dust from the eruption of Mount Pinatubo in the Phillipines. This blew in 1991 and has been linked with a one-fifth reduction in the ozone layer over Britain in 1992.

Of all the jargonistic terms that have baffled the environmental media, none ranks higher these days than 'ozone holes'. Ozone is a rich form of oxygen lying in the stratosphere between 15 and 40km above the earth surface. This layer serves many functions including that of reducing the amount of ultraviolet light passing down to affect the oceans' primary plant life, crop yields and even the incidence of some skin cancers. In 1985 the Antarctic 'Ozone Hole' was first reported, though massive losses of ozone had occurred there since the early 1970s. In the very cold stratispheres over the polar regions, rather dense clouds form in which chlorofluorocarbons (CFCs) are broken down to produce active and noxious chlorine compounds which deplete the ozone in the presence of sunlight. It seems that even over Britain the ozone loss may amount to 2% over the past 20 years. Most of the CFCs are used in foams, refrigerators and aerosols, and it is no wonder that the European Union is seeking to phase out all non-essential uses of CFCs by 1997. Just a 10% thinning of the ozone layer will give a 25% increase in global skin cancer.

Most pollution-related problems in the mountains are more tangible. In the recent past, concern focused on smoke and sulphur dioxide pollution, but this has declined and instead worries have shifted to high rates of nitrate deposition. This century has witnessed something like a four-fold increase in this, and even over the Greenland Icecap nitrate concentrations in snowfall have doubled. Most of the mountain air stream comes from the Atlantic, but there are variants, notably from the polluted south and east as far as the Baltic. Something like 30% of the cloud or rain-borne deposition of pollutants is attributed to only 3-8% per cent of wet days. Part of the problem here is that mountain plants rely heavily on atmospheric nitrogen for growth. They are supremely adapted for exploiting nitrogen and other nutrients from rainfall and the atmosphere but are, therefore, extremely sensitive to even small changes in this supply because of pollution.

The woolly fringe moss that carpets the northern and western mountain summits gets its nutrients from clouds and, to a lesser extent, from rainfall. Because cloud cover is greater higher up, and clouds trap and then concentrate pollutants, the clouds actually have concentrations of pollutants three to five times greater than in rainfall. The moss imbibes these pollutants and, not surprisingly, has been found with high tissue nitrogen levels on the south-eastern Highland tops as well as south of the Highlands – close to major sources from industrial pollution, sheep farms and conurbations. Indeed, research comparing mountain mosses collected last century and stored in herbaria with samples collected in the 1990s, has revealed three to five-fold increases in tissue concentrations of nitrogen. There is mounting evidence that acidic deposition is damaging mountain vegetation, notably in alliance with heavy grazing pressures, though more so in Wales and England than in Scotland. Recently published work revealed that some 30% of upland plant communities are vulnerable to pollution – about 60% of them occurring in the high mountains. The latest research, by Dr Clare Woolgrove and Dr Sarah Woodin at Aberdeen University, has shown pollution to be damaging 'late' snowbeds. Now these are remarkable gems of communities, with mosses and lichens that have snow packed over them for up to 10 months of the year. Their total extent amounts to only 250 hectares in Scotland, in the highest of the central and western Highland hills. There are .records of 'black snow' in the Cairngorms, with the carbon and fly ash known to have originated from

'Looking across to Ben Nevis and its legions...there is a slight haziness to the view.'

COIRE CAS, CAIRN GORM – With the clutter of a modern down-hill ski development.

eastern Europe as well as from the Central Belt. Snow is an efficient scavenger of pollutants, releasing these in an 'acid flush' as the snow melts in late spring and summer. On Bidean nam Bian and Lochnagar, this century, there have been significant increases in tissue nitrogen levels in their characteristic snowbed mosses. Moreover, critical loads for nitrogen (set by government as the maximum rate of deposition by pollutants which can be endured indefinitely without adverse effects on ecosystems) are exceeded considerably in snowbeds. Although there are controls over emissions from power stations and cars – the major sources of nitrate pollutants – these may not be sufficiently stringent to protect the snowbeds.

Skiing Developments, Recreation and Erosion

Whilst France, Austria, Switzerland, Canada and the USA have substantial skiing industries compared with ours, here in Scotland there has been a 10% increase per annum in skiing activity. This is pleasing for few sports match the exhilaration offered by travel *en piste*, and in its special way off-*piste*. The problem lies with the paraphernalia of the chairlifts, ski-tows, snow fences, car parks and outhouses, not so much in their impact on ecology but more on the landscape, and on the beauty and formerly untamed nature of the high land.

Skiing began in Scotland in 1890 following its introduction from Norway. It was in the late 1940s that organised skiing began here, with hoteliers in Speyside offering skiing as an extra. In 1956 the Glencoe development on Meall a'Bhuiridh began, and by 1962 there were two more commercial developments – at Cairnwell and Cairn Gorm – followed later by the Lecht and Aonach Mor. Ben Lawers was popular back in the 1930s, especially by the Lochan na Lairige, though since then interest has been much greater elsewhere.

Damage to the high ground has arisen from several facets: that caused by past construction using heavy-tracked vehicles, with consequent gully erosion and slumping; erection of fences to prolong snow cover that also alters the natural character of habitats; bruising, tearing and cutting of plants by skis on areas where snow cover is shallow or incomplete; and the erection of pylons with overhead wires which become eyesores and kill low-flying ptarmigan and red grouse. Helicopters have been used for the most recent developments, however, and attention to caring detail in minimising damage is commendable.

The knock-on effects of these developments, notably on Cairn Gorm, are considerable, with massively more people uplifted or attracted to the tops. In the Cairngorms, that brilliant field ecologist, Dr Adam Watson, has undertaken some of the most far-sighted and demanding monitoring of environmental change anywhere in Britain. He has demonstrated the creeping, widening and lengthening of footpaths since the early 1960s, and the expansion of erosion (as opposed to the natural harsh weathering of soils and plants). Between 1944-59 and 1962-88 there have been increases in numbers of people by sixty-fold on Cairn Gorm, compared with only seven to thirteen-fold on other high tops without skiing developments in the Cairngorms. These are fragile places and the granitic soils of Cairn Gorm, in particular, yield readily to boot and wind. The birds, it seems, can tolerate some heavy disturbance, but even the confiding dotterel may desist from breeding when harried by scores of photographers or inadvertently disturbed by hundreds of walkers on a warm summer's day. There are also the food scraps and other accompaniments of man that initially attract crows, and in some areas possibly gulls, that in turn depredate nests and young of ptarmigan and dotterel.

Scotland has five ski centres, with Aonach Mor the latest to be developed. Various studies have examined the potential for expanding these centres or developing others such as Ben Wyvis and Drumochter. Work continues to explore various options, and even satellite imagery has been employed by researchers at the University of Edinburgh to quantify the extent and condition of snow cover.

Surely though it is the clutter on Cairn Gorm and ugly fences and pylons on Glas Maol that betray the worst of these schemes. This is wholly out of place in such natural wild areas. The balancing act is near-impossible. Many of the people benefitting from chairlifts, paths and even alpine restaurants would not otherwise reach such heights. But then there are scarcely enough places anywhere in Britain without the hand of man. So why here, in our only truly arctic-alpine wilderness, should the mountain soul be wounded by shards of development?

Now we also have hang-gliding, para-gliding and even parachuting on or off the hills. The upsurge in mountain biking is remarkable, posing special problems for hill manager and walker. Walkers, climbers and mountaineers are more numerous – many of the former with dogs. There seem to be many problems here, ranging from the massive growth and proliferation of tracks and paths (and, of course, signs), the spread of erosion, putative disturbance of nesting birds, interference with grouse shooting and disturbance of deer sought by stalkers; and broader issues touching on who can go where and impediments to access. Other forms of disturbance include the illegal plundering of birds' eggs and collecting of rarer plants. Then there is the insidious bulldozing of tracks and dependence on all terrain vehicles off-track, all apparently to render the hill tamer for shooting and managing stock.

Numbers of people on the hills these days defy belief. For instance, 60,000 scale Ben Lomond annually, and it is now common to see at least a score of walkers on most of our Munros on a day in summer. Damage to paths is a growing concern, with the steepness, roughness and wetness of the ground affecting the degree of erosion. Pioneer work on path construction and restoration of damaged land has been undertaken by Dr Bob Aitken and Dr Neil Bayfield. This points the way to how important parts can be rehabilitated. But the costs are considerable, with £20 per metre needed to rebuild a path (£40 where stone pitching is used). Nevertheless, footpath 'users' contribute a lot to the local economy: one recent study in Ross and Cromarty found that the equivalent of over 250 full-time jobs are supported by hikers.

Recently, there has been much debate about the extent and causes of erosion in the uplands. Research at the University of Stirling suggests peat erosion is common in the Highlands – notably in the Monadhliaths and further east and in Shetland – whereas gullies and landslip scars are more widespread. Many reported cases of peat erosion have beginnings some 20-50 years ago, whereas gullies and scars may have been more recent and, principally, linked with grazing. There is great potential for more work here, exploring changes this century as well as over hundreds of years.

Clutter, erosion and mess are the stamps of disrespect, as much for the hills as for the people who love them. And what complexities touch at the very spirit of freedom. Why even the fear of confrontation with an irate owner or keeper compels some to use familiar routes not best suited to minimising impact on land or its beauty. Here are great imponderables: matching enjoyment with restraint, promoting appreciation and fitness with concern and care, and unleashing that roaming spirit of joy.

It is appropriate here to end our sketch of land-use change and man's impacts on these special places. Much of the land has a more tired appearance now, yielding more readily to people and tracks, grazing and burning, the car park and pollution. Perhaps just a century ago it sprang back after the garron and its burden passed, held back more of its water and boggy slurry, and yielded more to the eye and ear. At least more people now appreciate the importance of the key environmental and recreational features – some of which time has stolen forever.

A lone Scots pine. Will the slopes of our mountains begin to recover what has been lost?

A Journey

I love the haunts of solitude
The coverts of the free
Where man ne'er ventures to intrude
And God gives peace to me
Where all I hear and all I see
In peace of freedom roam
Here shall my heart's own dwelling be
And find itself at home.

John Clare, *A Song*, 1793-1864

THE TORRIDON MOUNTAINS (opposite) – There is no place quite like Scotland and no land quite like its mountains.

THE AONACH EAGACH RIDGE AND MOUNTAINS OF GLENCOE

A Journey

There is poetry in the qualities of the mountains, and to each of us our exploration provides a sense of uplift never the same on different occasions or in different places.

From an ecological perspective there are some magnificent contrasts and parallels. In the Southern Uplands, the Galloway and Carrick Hills resemble the Lewisian gneiss lunar scape of the north-western Highlands. Here are rocky and rugged southern outliers of the western Highlands not found in the Lake District or north Wales. Little treats are tucked away here: scarce nesting dotterel, a few breeding golden eagles, ravens and black-throated divers but, surprisingly, no breeding greenshanks. Here also are the most southerly patterned hummock-pool bog systems, with the Silver Flowe quite outstanding. The high summit heaths are mainly grassy with stiff sedge and woolly fringe moss. Bilberry-lichen heaths smother the high flanks where, in the North-West Highlands, there is a richness of mosses, prostrate heather and black bearberry. Towards the north-east the rolling plateaux and steep-sided glens and cloughs of the Moffat Hills and Broad Law are more akin to the north of England and Wales, though the soils are slightly better. The grouse moors here are rich, and just some 20 miles to the north-east the Moorfoots have an abundance of red grouse and golden plover. This part of Scotland has virtually no surviving stands of natural montane vegetation however. The prevailing grassy and highly afforested ground bears witness to excessive pressures from grazing sheep and conifer tree planting, though the grouse moors are superb.

Moving into the south-western Highlands we find, south of the Great Glen, some of the highest mountains – at around or above 3,600 feet – encircling an area with granites, Dalradian schists and, at the north end, Moine rocks. Moving clockwise there is Ben Cruachan, Ben Nevis and the Mamores, Creag Meagaidh, Ben Alder, Ben Lawers over to Beinn Heasgarnich, and further still Ben Lui, and finally Ben More and Stob Binnein. The rocks – hard and soft, base-rich and somewhat poor – profer an exceptional diversity of mountain plants and vegetation. Here only are the most south-westerly vestiges of the middle alpine zone comparable with much grander vistas of this zone in western Norway. Ben Nevis, Aonach Mor, Creag Meagaidh and Ben Alder are exceptional in this respect yet even in the Breadalbanes the arctic flora is poor compared with that on kindred Norwegian hills, but at least one gains a vivid impression of former glories.

To the west are lower hills which, geologically, end north on Rum and south on Arran and the Mull of Kintyre. The vegetation is principally blanket bog and damp heath. The Tertiary basalts and ultrabasic rocks on Rum, Morvern and Mull (Ardmeanach) are particularly interesting in providing a rich refugium for base-rich loving mountain plants.

Generally though, the more notable habitats and animals are better represented farther north and on the mainland proper. North of the Great Glen there is the dissected spine of the ancient Highland watershed, and off this the spectacularly rocky ridges and pinnacles west of the Moine Thrust Plane. Along the watershed, the exciting hills stretch from Carn Eighe, Mam Sodhail and Sgurr na Lapaich north of Loch Affric (the Affric-Cannich Hills) up over Monar Forest to the Fannichs, Beinn Dearg and north still to Ben More Assynt. This is a diverse assortment of hills with large high summit or shoulder plateaux and mixtures of oceanic and more continental boggy and montane habitats. Beinn Dearg and Seana Bhraigh have the most northern complete sequence of late lying snowbeds in Britain, and Ben More Assynt has the most northern of these. Whilst south of the Great Glen there were more lichens in the heathery and bilberry montane heaths, here there is much more woolly fringe moss and bearberry, and the snowbeds are relatively large.

Westwards and northwards, beyond the Moine Thrust Plane, are the scoured and wettest of hills. These are steep and rocky with limited areas of very high ground compared with those just viewed to the east. Their appearance is at once familiar to the hill-goer – cloaks of white and grey summit crags and screes, lower brownish heathery crags and, at the foot, pale green purple moor grass-infested wet heaths. Here, the Torridonian sandstone mountains rest on Lewisian gneiss, and away from these stretches the characteristic striated knobbly and lochan-studded landscape. The hills run northwards from Sgurr na Ciche at the head of Loch Nevis, through Beinn Bhan on Applecross, the mighty Liathach, Beinn Eighe and Beinn Alligin, the Letterewe giants rising out by Loch Maree, An Teallach, Cul Mor and Cul Beag just north of the Coigach, and finally to the shattered tops of Foinaven and Arkle. These all share the same raw scree-shrouded appearance and have wet heaths of heather, woolly fringe moss and juniper. These hills are unique.

Some of the lower tops outwith the Torridonian peaks also merit note. There is the Trotternish ridge on Skye with its massive landslips, and the rockiest of all places – North Harris (Clisham) and indeed parts of South Harris. It is in areas here that montane communities come down to their lowest elevation. Sgribhis-Bheinn (only 371m, 1,216') close to Cape Wrath is remarkable in its harshness of windswept ground, resembling that of Ronas Hill on Shetland, and Ward Hill on Hoy, Orkney.

East of Foinaven we find Ben Hope, and just to the south Ben Hee, Ben Klibreck, and Ben Armine, which have more vegetation in common with the more western rugged hills than with their flat-topped neighbours to the south. It is the prevailing oceanic climate from the west at work here, with mist, rain and wind extending their influence from the west coast. Here, the jagged-ridged Ben Loyal is a fascinating exception to the above list, for it is composed of the igneous rock syenite – a particularly acidic one that supports an especially restricted flora.

Remember our link between Galloway (with the Merrick hills) and the vaster wilds of the north-west. But behold the bonuses up in the north-west. There are regular breeding black-throated divers and many more red-throats on the myriad dubh lochans. Ptarmigan abound on the tops with dotterel, and even occasional nesting snow buntings. Below we see and hear more of the bog-dwelling waders – greenshank, rare wood sandpiper, and if you are very lucky – purple sandpiper, ruff and red-necked phalarope. There are also great and arctic skuas (expanding southwards gradually from their arctic maritime heath and bog strongholds), and here also even great black-backed gulls breed on the hill. Why, even the other birds seem more ebullient here, with golden plover, dunlin, and common snipe abundant and noisy, and golden eagles, ravens, merlin and peregrine seen much more frequently.

Now we move south again, to the eastern and central Highlands where we find more treats and surprises. But first, in Caithness, steal a look at conical Morven and the lower quartzite saddle of Scaraben. Then travel down over Beinn Dorain by Brora, Carn Salachaidh and other sharp peaks west of Ardgay, to Ben Wyvis – the highest of the more eastern hills in the north. These hills have more bogs with heather and bog cotton, and the heaths have more lichens relative to mosses. Ben Wyvis confounds the comparison in some ways. Whilst it is indeed less oceanic in character than Beinn Dearg to the west, but similar in some ways to the Affric-Cannich Hills, it has a massive plateau carpeted deeply in woolly fringe moss and stiff sedge. A heavy cloud typically hangs over here, just as it is characteristic over the Ben Hope summit peak, with the mossy carpet petering out just below the cloud-line.

So we come upon the massif of the highest mountains in Britain. Here are familiar friends – the great tableland of the Monadhliath, and that granite mass of the Cairngorms. To come upon Cairn Gorm from north of Aviemore is breathtaking. Here are the 'Northern Corries' – bold and magnificent. The geology of this land divides into the southern Dalradian and northern Moine series of metamorphic rocks. There are schists, gneisses, quartzites and huge granitic intrusions. In appearance these are mainly with undulating high plateaux, deeply dissected by steep-walled troughs cut by the Grampian Ice Sheets which tracked north-eastwards. Below this greatest extent of 'middle-alpine' habitat in the British Isles lies productive grouse moor and the remnants in Deeside and Strathspey of their once glorious pine woodlands and associated birchwoods.

The high altitude, oceanic communities found in the west are less frequent here; instead we encounter massive late snowbeds and tawny-coloured heaths with three-leaved rush and woolly fringe moss. There are high altitude blanket bogs, in parts blackened and hagged, most noticeably in the Monadhliath, the western Cairngorms above Glen Feshie and on the east Drumochter plateaux. Wallowing deer may account for the eroding hags, though there is debate also about other potential causes – the cut and thrust effects of the Little Ice Age and acid pollution.

The better drained shoulders have woolly fringe moss, stiff sedge immediately below the bog, and bilberry-lichen heaths in sheltered areas with snow. These last communities are most akin to those on the more continental hills of the Alps and central Scandinavia. Lower down there are heathery lichen-rich heaths trailing down the wind-clipped spurs. Then there are steep slopes dominated by heather and bilberry-grass heaths, undulating towards the bottom where burning for red grouse is so evident. A drive through the Drumochter Pass north to Daviot shows off these lower hill features most beautifully. Note the absence of much rocky terrain, as most of the land is well vegetated. The screes on steep slopes add to the story of heavy burning and grazing, however, whilst the heathery drumlins – mounds of glacial drift – show off wonderfully just north of the Sow of Atholl.

You must pause by these places and appreciate their wealth and diversity. High up between Cairn Gorm and Ben Macdui there are late snowbeds spreading on to flat ground, yet elsewhere these are confined to gullies and sheltered steep slopes. There are corrie floors here with vegetation found towards the west on the highest summits. And there is no other place where the great, now spent force of ice, joins with wind to mould the vegetation to such extremes. An ascent through pinewoods adds to this special venture. Treat yourself to Rothiemurchus, and journey into Glen Einich or the Lairig Ghru; or try Glen Derry and Glen Quoich to the east – the last taking you up to Beinn a'Bhuird or farther still to Ben Avon. These are rich hills.

On a broader scale some contrasts begin to emerge among Scottish mountains. Important gradients of climate and plant life lie north-eastwards along the Dalradian hills, from as far as Ben Lawers and Meall nan Tarmachan in the west, to Caenlochan and Glen Clova in the relatively continental east. Some of the lower hills, with no high mountain vegetation, tie in with this gradient, with Shiehallion and Ben Vrackie as notable for this as for their affinities with the heathery hills of Orkney (West Mainland and Orphir-Stennes Hills).

At Drumochter there is a juncture between the oceanic Breadalbanes and the more continental Cairngorms, and even on the tops either side of the Pass this is apparent in the composition and patterning of plants. To the west, Creag Meagaidh and the massifs of Ben Alder and Aonach Mor are comparable, though more oceanic in character. To the north, the southern Monadhliath is somewhat similar to Drumochter, though slightly more continental in some features. Here are mossy-dominated heaths and bogs, whereas to the east there is also a good deal of dry lichen heaths. Yet we have to go to the Lecht, and other hills towards Inverness, for the rarer lichen-rich bogs. And so it goes on!

We have travelled with the clock hand and witnessed the west to east effects of variation in climate, and the differences northwards in wildlife and the impact of man. We have concentrated on the hills of greater biological importance, necessarily neglecting some of the more popular country such as the Trossachs and Ben Lomond, the Ochils, Campsie Fells and parts of Argyll. Yet for many who visit the mountains it is their beauty and wildness that commands affection. That is what is so tantalising – the direction and length of your journey depends as much on your outlook and starting point as on the nature of your quest and interest.

SUTHERLAND

"Sutherland – the South Land of the Norsemen – puts into Highland perspective talk of an overcrowded Britain. The hinterland of the far north-west, extending to the desolate magnificence of the Clo Mor sea cliffs near Cape Wrath and lonely Fionn Loch under the towering dome of Suilven, is a land of solitary splendour... Mountains, loch and glens of unrivalled beauty add a special poignancy to the occasional mound of stones marking the ruins of a crofting township." (Allan Campbell McLean, *Explore the Highlands and Islands,* 1976).

BEN LOYAL (opposite) and FOINAVEN (above) – two sentinels of the far north.

BEN STACK (Steep Hill, 721m)
The perfect symmetry of this conical hill affords spectacular views of Reay Forest, not least the vast scree-laden corries and ridges of Arkle. To the east, Creagan Meall Horn (729m) and the narrow, flat ridges of Sabhal Mor (702m) and Sabhal Beag (732m) take you to some of the quietest, high wilderness in the Highlands.

ARKLE (Hill of the Level Top, 787m) from the west, rising above the ancient plateau of Lewisian gneiss.

BEN HOPE (Hill of the Bay, 927m). Scotland's most northern Munro, with its prominent escarpment marking the north-west corner of 'The Flow Country'.

QUINAG (Cuinneag, Narrow-Mouthed Water Stoup, 764-808m)
Quinag lies between Loch Assynt and Loch a' Chairn Bhain,
standing at the head of the Torridonian sandstone chain of mountains that begin at Applecross. With three main summits it is one of the most striking mountains in Sutherland. It is steep too, with a cap of Cambrian quartzite.

SUILVEN

Whether it is seen from air or land this mountain is indomitable. Resembling a great broch from the west it is also often likened to a sugar loaf. No wonder Darling and Boyd in *The Highlands and Islands* exclaimed: 'There is only one Suilven and it is undoubtedly the most fantastic hill in Scotland.'
BEN MORE ASSYNT (998m) and CONIVAL (987m) from Glen Oykel (opposite).

Ross, Skye & The Outer Hebrides

"The complex and magical beauty of Ross numbs the imagination and mocks all attempts to describe it. In the first moments of an early dawn its great wastes and upthrust hills are grey with the pain of their solitude, and night-shadows still deepen the parallel lines on the troubled face of Liathach. The rising sun warms and enlivens, and at noon it glistens on the white quartzite head of Beinn Eighe. With the passing of day the ice-hewn spearheads on the side of Slioch are a gentle rose-pink above the blue mirror of Loch Maree, but southward the scarred sandstone flank of Beinn Alligin drips blood into the darkness of Torridon. The seasons change colour and metaphor." (John Prebble, *John Prebble's Scotland,* 1984)

Stac Pollaidh (613m, opposite) and Inverpolly National Nature Reserve from Knockan (above).

HARRIS

One can get no closer to the beginning of time than here, on North Harris, where the land is utterly rock-dominated – and has probably been so for several billion years. The highest hill, Clisham (799m) forms part of the Glen Scaladale Horseshoe, overlooking the majestic Loch Seaforth. In the west are the silvery sands of the Sound of Taransay, with a large peninsula holding Chaipaval. So much of the ground has been heavily burnt and grazed that we can only guess as to the former character of these oceanic mountains. There are affinities in vegetation with the mainland Lewisian and Moine hills, as well as with those on St Kilda. Don't be surprised if you see song thrushes in the mountains, for here and in the Uists they replace ring ouzels nesting high up on heathery boulder-fields.

AN TEALLACH (The Forge, 1,062m)

BEINN EIGHE (File Hill, 1,010m). Vast quartzite scree fields drape the southern flanks of Britain's first designated National Nature Reserve.

LOCH MAREE AND SLIOCH – The mountain is virtually impregnable around three-quarters of its body.

THE BEINN DEARG MASSIF FROM WEST OF LOCH GLASCARNOCH RESERVOIR

Just north of Dirrie More is the most northern high mountain country in Britain. The highest and most interesting summits include Beinn Dearg (1,084m), Seana Bhraigh (926m) to the north, and the great plateau of Am Faochagach (954m) above Loch Vaich. One can approach these hills from Loch Broom, from Strath Oykel, or even from Gleann Mor where the River Carron begins its journey to the Kyle of Sutherland.

Richard Gilbert, in his book on *200 Challenging Walks in Britain and Ireland* (1990), was perhaps the first to point out that a walk from Loch Broom to the Dornoch Firth takes the narrowest line on land between western and eastern Britain.

These are fantastic hills, rated by botanists as bettered only by the Clova mountains and Ben Lawers massif. Look out for the small shrub dwarf birch (*Betula nana*) – virtually confined to the Highlands, but growing here extensively in the wetter, boggy parts. And on the tops you will encounter an abundance of pink-flowered thrift and moss campion. Look also at the wind-blasted and frost-heaved spurs that seem to come alive in the setting sun. The diversity of plant communities and richness of flora is unrivalled in the northern Highlands, and there are treats of rare mammals and breeding birds characteristic of high, open and remote deer forest.

THE BLACK CUILLIN, ISLE OF SKYE

In the Cuillin there is an utterly treacherous formation of ridges, pinnacles, corries and glaciated hollows surrounding the crucible of Loch Coruisk. The land is savage and the weather has a temperament to match it.

THE BLACK CUILLIN RIDGE, ISLE OF SKYE

The main ridge is almost 1,000m high. Its gabbro landscape has massive cliffs, smooth slabs and razor-sharp ridges, with the rock visibly eroded by the elements. Many of the possible climbs require considerable skill and experience but are rewarded by privileged panoramic views towards the mainland and other islands, and of the Black Cuillin itself. Looking from the air towards the spur of Gars-Bheinn (opposite).

BEN WYVIS (Awesome Hill or perhaps Hill of Terror, 1,046m) from the air.
This 'whaleback' has Glas Leatchad Mor (aptly translated as 'big greenish-grey slope')
as its highest summit. Often with a cap of cloud, Ben Wyvis has the most extensive single carpet
of woolly fringe moss summit heath anywhere in Britain.

LIATHACH (The Grey One) from the air – with its awesome, terraced ramparts (opposite).

Kintail, Knoydart & The Inner Isles

NORTHERN RIDGES OF THE FIVE SISTERS OF KINTAIL

This is one of the grandest of mountain ranges north of the Great Glen. Sgurr na Ciste Duibhe (1,027m) is one of the sisters' Munros – with its south face one of the highest and steepest in Britain. Behind to the north lies Beinn Fhadda (or Ben Attow 1,032m) running for almost 10km, and then the huge mountains of Carn Eighe (1,183m), Mam Sodhail (1,180m) and Sgurr nan Ceathreamhnan (1,151m). Looking across Strath Croe to the Mountains of Kintail (opposite).

LOCH AFFRIC

Looking across Loch Affric towards Sgurr na Lapaich.
Scattered remnants of the Caledonian Forest occur along the
Glen Affric floor, with birch and pine abundant. Many glen bottoms
would have appeared as this several thousand years ago – but the
flanks would have supported much more woodland and scrub.

GLEN BARRISDALE from the air, looking west towards the mountains of Knoydart.

RUM FROM ELGOL ON SKYE

The Rum Cuillin of five peaks (Hallival, Askival, Trallvall, Ainshval and Sgurr nan Gillean) compares well with its more celebrated 'black' neighbour on Skye. This island National Nature Reserve is owned by SNH, and is famed for many features including the reintroduction of sea eagles to Britain, the long-term study of red deer, Kinloch Castle, mountain-nesting Manx Shearwaters and clouds of midges. HALLIVAL and ASKIVAL from the sea (opposite). The reserve has been designated by UNESCO as a Biosphere Reserve.

GLEN NOE

The high pass of Glen Noe, at 579m, links Loch Etive and Loch Awe.
Northwards are Beinn a'Chochuill (980m) and Beinn Eunaich (989m) joined by a bealach of 728m. Beyond is the great bulk of Ben Starav (1,078m) and Glas Bheinn Mhor (997m).
Upper Lorn has some of the most remote and barren high country in Scotland.

BEN CRUACHAN from the air – a complex mass of ridges (opposite).

BEN MORE (Big Hill, 966m), MULL

On this second largest of the Inner Hebridean islands is the only island Munro outside Skye. The boulder-splattered ridges contrast perfectly with the grassy and wet heath glens that run into the sea. The Ross of Mull viewed from on high over Loch Scridain has superb stands of hazel scrub. As an extra you may see eagles here.

THE PAPS OF JURA (Deer Island)

It was below these hills that George Orwell wrote *Nineteen Eighty-Four*. The highest peak, Beinn An Oir (784m), is clad by a torn blanket of scree. The climate is mild and there are close affinities with the oceanic fringe of western Ireland. You have a wonderful sense of remoteness here, with the Sound of Jura to the east and the Sound of Islay to the west.

BEN NEVIS (opposite), AND BUACHAILLE ETIVE MÓR, GLENCOE (right)

Britain's highest mountain, Ben Nevis, is claimed to have been discovered by the Hopkinson family in 1892. Imagine their excitement on first seeing the Tower Ridge and North-East Buttress. 'The Ben' has one of the grandest cliffs in Britain (over 600m high).

If you can, avoid the popular route from the west, for you miss out on the massive scale of this giant. The summit top is extensive and flat, covered mainly by boulder fields. It was reputed to have had a permanent snow patch, and a unique series of meteorological recordings were made by the former Meteorological Observatory (built in 1883 and closed in 1904). The rocks include a mix of granites, schists, quartzite and limestone that favour a rich flora. The Ben has tracts of rocky and relatively inaccessible ground about which surprisingly little is known of the plants. Only recently, for instance, did researchers discover an abundance of mountain avens associated with a rich alpine flora. There may be some surprises yet.

Glencoe to the south is steeped in history and is a magnet for mountaineers. Bidean nam Bian has superb hanging valleys and other features that excite geomorphologists. Not so widely acknowledged is the botany: the cliffs are generally acidic rhyolite, but there are numerous outcrops of calcareous andesite with a rich flora.

LOCH LOMOND – With its woody islands and Scotland's most southern Munro, Ben Lomond.

THE TROSSACHS

For many people the Trossachs are the Highlands in miniature, helped by associations with the redoubtable Rob Roy MacGregor. Luxuriant forests of birch attest to rich upland soils, with the highest hill being Ben Ledi (879m).

THE COBBLER (Ben Arthur, 884m)
The three chunky peaks of The Cobbler top Scotland's most popular 'little' mountain.
It is best climbed from Arrochar station – after a leisurely journey up the West Highland Line to the head of Loch Long.

BEN LUI or Beinn Laoigh (1,130m) from Beinn Dubhchraigh – black rock hill (opposite).

THE GALLOWAY HILLS ABOVE GLEN TROOL

The Merrick (843m) is the highest hill in the Southern Uplands. The lower land is granitic, rugged, boggy moorland, rising to the more rounded Ordovician rock tops. The extensive north-facing cliffs have several interesting patches of montane vegetation. The Rhinns of Kells, to the east of Glen Trool, are slightly lower – Corserine and Carlin's Cairn have the most southern good quality montane *Racomitrium lanuginosum* heaths in Britain.

CAIRNSMORE OF FLEET surrounded by forestry (opposite).

TINTO (left) AND THE LOWTHER HILLS (opposite)

Tinto (707m) is a volcanic outlier often visible from the west of Glasgow, and named after its red felsite.

The Lowthers, directly south, have 15 hills over 610m. The two highest are Lowther Hill (725m) and Green Lowther (732m) – both typical of the rolling hills in this region.

This is sheep country, and amongst the hills there are ample signs of heavy grazing by sheep. The dwarf shrubs of heather and bilberry, grazed repeatedly, have been replaced by grasses, and bracken on the richer, freely drained slopes. The common dominants are aptly named sheep's fescue, wavy hair grass, bents and vernal grass, with mat grass and heath rush on the wetter soils. Locally, the heather is holding out – but only just. Where there is less grazing pressure (and perhaps, also, less burning) straggling heather exists.

But the heather can make a comeback... When sheep are removed or reduced considerably in number the bents and sheep's fescue will be overwhelmed by heather again in 10-15 years. Bracken, on the other hand, can obstruct heather growth for decades.

Near Wanlockhead there are good examples of muirburn for the benefit of red grouse: this sustains heather cover. Yet over the Southern Uplands as a whole, some 40% of heather cover has been lost since the 1940s, to forestry as well as grazing sheep.

The Breadalbanes & Forest of Atholl

LOOKING SOUTH ABOVE BLAIR ATHOLL

The Farragon Hills to the west stand out on high hill country reaching west to Schiehallion. There are several mines here for the mineral barytes. Ben Vrackie, just to the east, stands sentinel over the south-eastern Highlands and has a rich flora, particularly in the broken crags of Dalradian schists, with grouse moor comprising much of the lower habitat.

SCHIEHALLION, the fairy hill of the Caledonians, and Loch Tummel from the Queen's View (opposite).

LOCH AN DAIMH, GLEN LYON

The Breadalbanes, with their thick beds of rich rocks, are a botanical paradise. South of Ben Nevis, Ben Lawers (1,214m) is the highest mountain in Britain – falling barely short of 4,000'. Of all our mountains this is the richest for arctic-alpine plants on account of its fertile soils. Ben Ghlas and Meall nan Tarmachan (1,042m) are also very good – notably the lush, tall herb ledges along the Creag an Lochain. The invertebrate fauna is also varied, the area being well-known for its molluscs, and as the Scottish headquarters of the small mountain ringlet butterfly.

THE EASTERN BREADALBANE HILLS (opposite).

Rannoch, Drumochter & Badenoch

THE MOUNTAINS OF DRUMOCHTER

Drumlins in Coire Dhomain (above). Just west of the A9 between the Sow of Atholl and the Boar of Badenoch these terrific, hummocky moraines stand out. Look up to Sgairneach Mhor (Big Stony Hillside, 991m) and Beinn Udlamain (Gloomy Mountain, 1,010m) and you can imagine the last retreat of a small glacier – spawning these mounds of debris. There are other good examples in Glen Geusachan and Glen Eidart in the Cairngorms.

The silhouette of A'MHARCONAICH (975m) purple with heather in bloom (opposite).

CREAG MEAGAIDH (Bogland Rock, 1,130m)

Looking into Moy Corrie (above). This magnificent mountain is a National Nature Reserve, purchased by the Nature Conservancy Council in 1985. Its north-eastern Coire Ardair (opposite) has cliffs 300m high. The vegetation now demonstrates various sequences of habitats from the low ground with mosaics of woodland, heath, grassland and bog, to fine sub-alpine and alpine heaths on the mid slopes, finally to summit moss-heaths and snow-bed vegetation on the high plateau. Birch woodland, with scattered willows, rowans, alders and aspens, generally extends up to around 450m and in places to 600m. Profuse regeneration of woodland and scrub is evident following the removal of red deer.

BEN ALDER (1,148m)
The vast tableland of Ben Alder beyond Loch Ericht from Beinn Udlamain where the range of heaths, alpine grasslands and late snow beds is tremendous. Look out for the superbly colourful mosses in bubbling springs and flushes with an abundance of some characteristic of limestone. The bleak northern edge of Rannoch Moor, with Leum Uilleim (906m) and Beinn a'Bhric (876m) above Corrour (opposite).

The Cairngorms & Eastern Grampians

"We love the Cairngorms and have chosen to work in them for decades. They are unique in Britain for the great expanse of ground over 3,000 feet and thus for the extent and richness of their arctic-like plateaux, corries, lochs, soils, vegetation and animals... The Cairngorms have reached the crunch. The politicians and civil servants must create an overall plan, or these great hills, as we have known them, will perish. What the nation must do, and do urgently, is to create a body with real teeth and powers of 'yea' and 'nay', and commend it to conserve and develop, strictly in that order." (D. Nethersole-Thompson and A. Watson, *The Cairngorms*, 1981)

THE NORTHERN CAIRNGORMS from Lynebreck (opposite). LURCHER'S GULLY and the Northern Corries (above).

ABOVE THE CAIRN GORM PLATEAUX, LOOKING EAST TOWARDS LOCHNAGAR

The flanks of the vast Cairn Gorm, Ben Macdui and Braeriach plateaux have fantastic glacial and periglacial landforms; look at the sheets, terraces, lobes and bumps of boulders and rock debris. Some of the smaller features were probably active during the last few thousand years. Being there is to appreciate the natural forces that have moulded the landscape.

AN GARBH CHOIRE between Braeriach and Cairn Toul – An ethereal dawn.

BEN AVON (opposite) AND LOCHNAGAR (above)

Viewed from the north you get hints of the complexity of Ben Avon (1,171m), for this is Britain's most massive mountain – having more ground above 900m than any other. The giant granite tors are ancient features dating back many millions of years. Perhaps these escaped the shroud of ice that consumed the Cairngorms during the Ice Age. There are huge shoulders on the mountain; those to the north are especially exposed with large stands of scattered tussocks of three-leaved rush set in barren granite grit and rock.

LOOKING TOWARDS THE MONADHLIATH FROM LURCHER'S CRAG

In the Monadhliath Mountains there is a high desolate watershed of bog – much of it with substantial erosion gullies. This is uncharted country with a rich mixture of oceanic and more continental habitats, and good populations of nesting waders.

The triple-buttressed north end of CARN ETCHACHAN ends the journey above Loch Avon (opposite).

Revelation

Little by little, as when a man climbs a mountain the earth unfolds beneath him so for yourselves ye shall see and know, needing no testimony from another, no, not even from ancient scripture... For the kingdom of Heaven is within you.

W. H. Murray, *Mountaineering in Scotland*, 1947

We need a clear vision for the mountains. Since the post-war era of the 1940s and 1950s, many who share this concern have produced major treatises on protecting and improving, or simply enjoying the Highlands. They range from ecologists such as Derek Ratcliffe, Adam Watson, J. Morton Boyd and Donald McVean, environmental historians such as Chris Smout, John and Hilary Birks, Kevin Edwards and Paul Ramsay, more 'popular' writers like Bill Murray, Jim Crumley, Chris Bonington, Hamish Brown, Cameron McNeish, Richard Gilbert and Donald Bennet, and those anxious to find the right niche for man as part of the wilds – Jim Hunter and Michael Wigan provide two contrasts.

It is also quite remarkable how many people hark back to the writings of Fraser Darling, who may have provided the stimulus for later works, having captured so poignantly the plight of the wilder parts of Scotland. Scots-born John Muir, founding father of the environmental management of mountain environments in the USA, is another 'visionary' eulogized by many.

Some of these individuals have a canvas of Scotland on which they paint in the colours and textures of the landscapes, habitats, wildlife and settlements which form their image for action. If only they could agree!

One vision is that of a revitalised mountain land where, in each region and within every zone, the more natural habitats are given a chance of full expression. I am repeatedly disappointed by the poor stature of our vegetation, and the many signs of heavy grazing, burning and erosion. In many parts the exposure of rocks, screes and bare ground is greater than would have been seen in earlier centuries, and this seems to stem from the stripping away of plant life and associated soil processes. Only a few centimetres of soil and plants may separate the bedrock from the elements of nature. Yet we take this for granted and seem surprised when the land fails the fertility test and gradually loses its plant cover.

On many of the northern and western hills it is likely that substantial areas of wet heath and bog have been lost, leaving what for many is an attractive, rugged and of course rocky landscape. In less harsh regions and on drier habitats, the commoner grasses dominate, disguising the loss of natural biodiversity. I look to wooded islands on lochs, grazing-free cliffs and scree fields – areas which have not been recently disturbed – as well as to comparable habitats abroad in making these observations. Repeated visits to mountain summits reinforce my view that the moss, lichen and dwarf-shrub cover *can* be restored to provide a more diverse landscape. What we see now on some of the high tops in the Lake District may soon be seen in the Scottish Highlands –

SUILVEN – From the west it is known as *Caisteal Liath*, 'The Grey Castle'.

if grazing pressures are not reduced.

Lower down, more effort is needed to restore dwarf herbs (forbs) to montane grasslands and heaths on basic soils. And why not encourage the restoration of tall scrub (juniper, willow and birch) to its upper altitudinal limit, as appropriate to geology and soils? It is surprising how much blanket bog has limited cover of bog mosses (Sphagnum). This is attributable to burning, grazing and perhaps exacerbated by acid deposition. Some of the other communities would benefit from maintenance and enhancement, such as the near-natural alpine acidic grasslands and snowbed communities, the alpine and sub-alpine calcareous grasslands, alpine dwarf-herb communities, the range of acidic to calcareous mires and springs, and the attractive tall-herb and fern-rich communities, including those of rocky habitats. These all form a part of the wonderful tapestry of the mountains -- but work is needed both to restore its fabric and ensure its longevity.

There is a richness and diversity in this landscape of mountains – from rolling hills to rugged peaks, steep glens to mountain lochs, and from the land to the sea with its many islands. Yet we have lost our trees and many of our heaths, and smothered some of our greatest bogs with plantations. Stony heaps and old 'lazy' beds mark the eviction of a people and the loss of a culture once married to the land. Sheep and deer now roam the hill, their numbers often out of kilter with habitats on which they depend. Bulldozed tracks, ragged paths and contemporary artifacts breach and scar the wild tops – helping some but offending others.

Many questions come to mind. Should more people be attracted and sustained for their leisure? Should pristine spots be zoned for conservation? Or must we leave these divisive elements and forces alone – to come and go as the whim of nature and man decree?

Everywhere in the world the rural mountain economy is marginal, and in Scotland it seems it is no different. Agriculture is the mainstay land-use. Although it delivers social and economic benefits, it does not always benefit the land. Some huge estates managed for sport have more resources to rely on, and can portray an image of restricted use and care. Developers, of course, eagerly seek out opportunities, and visitors come, some bearing wealth for those who are dependent on them. There are those who hold that wilderness and wildlife belong to an altogether higher order and merit unprecedented conservation. Somehow, all of these activities must continue, but on resources which are scarce.

The stakeholders are plenty – owners, occupiers and managers of the land, Local Authorities, voluntary organisations such as the World Wide Fund for Nature, Royal Society for the Protection of Birds, John Muir Trust, National Trust for Scotland, major representative bodies such as the National Farmers Union for Scotland, Scottish Landowners Federation, and Government agencies such as Highlands and Islands Enterprise, the Forestry Commission, Historic Scotland and Scottish Natural Heritage. These bodies are clearly there to influence others in achieving broad environmental goals and to lead on an agenda for action.

Yet if we are to promote care of the mountains we have to tackle the issues at scales ranging from international to local. At the former level there are European Union Directives on birds, and, more recently, on habitats. There will be Special Protection Areas for birds and Special Areas of Conservation for habitats and other species (together called 'Natura 2000' sites, to symbolise the conservation of important natural resources by the year 2000 – and beyond). Some of these areas will embrace key mountain habitats such as the alpine and sub-alpine heaths, montane acid grasslands dominated by mosses and sedges, and the more local mountain willow scrub, alpine calcareous grasslands and plants dwelling in acid rock crevices and scree fields. And there will be more protection for some populations of golden eagle and merlin, golden plover and dotterel, and others deemed rare or endangered in Europe. The World Heritage Convention adopted by UNESCO in 1972 and ratified by our Government in 1984, recognises the outstanding international elements of our cultural and natural heritage. In Scotland, only St Kilda has been listed as a World Heritage Site, but the

LIATHACH, Torridon in the glow of the setting sun.

Cairngorms have been nominated for listing.

In June 1992, most of the world's leaders met in Rio de Janeiro for the Earth Summit. There, two major reports were tabled on the global condition of the mountains: 'The State of the World's Mountains – A Global Report' and 'An Appeal for the Mountains: Mountain Agenda'. From within the UK, the Scottish Highlands alone were mentioned in these, with concern expressed about the pattern of ownership, the role of agriculture and the scant expenditure on mountain areas.

We now have 'Agenda 21' setting out the actions for environmental and economic conduct for the nations of the world into the twenty-first century.

Worldwide there are some 430 protected mountain areas, and these will initially attract most attention. The UK 'Biodiversity Action Plan' published as a command paper in 1994 sets out the government's plans as part of the follow-up to the Rio summit. A provisional agenda for mountain areas has been prepared for government, with far-reaching recommendations on agricultural reform. This, together with the proposals for 'Natura 2000' sites, offers much greater protection for some mountain areas. Even in the non-designated areas, habitats and wildlife should benefit through more sensitive management.

In Scotland, no single designation recognises the importance and needs of the mountains. The cornerstone of the existing approach involves targeting environmental grants through Environmentally Sensitive Areas, key landscape (National Scenic Areas) and nature conservation designations (Sites of Special Scientific Interest). Government has now announced the establishment of Natural Heritage Areas which will try to accommodate the range of interests across areas with outstanding landscapes, habitats and recreational values.

In October 1994, the International Union for the Conservation of Nature (IUCN) published a major proposal for protected areas in Europe. This urged the formal identification of areas in need of greatest protection (notably those proposed for national park status by the Countryside Commission for Scotland in 1990, as well as others) and development of the concept of Natural Heritage Areas.

Government-appointed Working Parties have considered the future of the Cairngorms and the Loch Lomond and Trossachs areas. Their report for the Cairngorms bears the hallmark of great progress in dialogue between interests. It recognises the majority of inimical issues, yet sets out, as a guiding principle, voluntary co-operation for future management. In essence, land managers are being urged to rally round a consensus of environmental stewardship. The Secretary of State for Scotland formally endorsed the report in Autumn 1994, and appointed David Laird as first chairman of the Cairngorms Partnership Board. Two priorities were set: to protect and enhance the core mountain zone, improving sympathetic management of recreation; and to protect, regenerate and re-establish native woodlands (notably the two great forests of Mar and Strathspey). The Board has begun to address these tasks, and the prospects for success seem greater than ever before. Over 60% of the Cairngorms is now owned or managed by conservation and/or public bodies, providing tremendous scope for action.

But should places such as the Cairngorms and the North-West Highlands have any land management, and in particular farming subsidies, delivering both environmental and social benefits? The answer should be a resounding yes.

Over 15% of Scotland now falls within Environmentally Sensitive Areas, and there are now Heather Moorland Scheme annual payments, with benefits conferred on low-lying hill areas, but not on the higher lands. The single greatest challenge is here, for in the future of agriculture rests the fate of the uplands as a whole. Deer estate managers are tackling the impacts of deer on hill and forest. Sweeping generalisations on reductions in deer numbers carry little credibility – instead, work is underway with local groups of deer managers, to determine where deer populations could be reduced to benefit habitat and wildlife.

For the mountains as a whole such a collaborative approach should work, but only where objectives are clear across Local Authority (or

Unitary Council) boundaries, and where sectoral policies are unified or at least co-ordinated. Here, bodies such as SNH, the RSPB and others, can demonstrate on land over which they have influence, what can be managed sustainably and dynamically, to promote and lead good practice by example. Present-day management of Creag Meagaidh, Beinn Eighe and Abernethy are examples of ideal management for conservation for instance.

Scotland has little wilderness in the strict sense – untouched by man, such as one finds in parts of the Arctic or Antarctic. But it has wild land a plenty. It is heartening to see many recent improvements in access provision and management. SNH has launched a 'Paths for All Initiative' and has helped establish an Access Forum which is bringing together representatives of recreational users, providers and statutory bodies. There are three key priorities: reducing impacts on the land and its wildlife; reducing confusion and improving confidence amongst all parties; and improving local access.

But let us return to the global scene, for the greatest environmental challenge is the advent of global warming and acidic pollution. There appears to be a scientific consensus that carbon dioxide concentrations will double and that surface air temperatures will rise by 2-5°C over the next 100 years. An increase of only 1°C is equivalent to a shift in mountain vegetation 200-300km northwards and 150-200 metres upwards. Already mountain glaciers are retreating on Baffin Island and in other parts of the high arctic, there has been a decrease in snow cover in North America, and in the Alps three-quarters of all glaciers are melting fast. But the past patterns of change, to say nothing about predictions for the future, are immensely complex.

By the year 2050 there may be a much higher frequency of mild winters. It seems, however, that there will be more winter snowfall, more rainfall, earlier snowmelt, and greater stream run-off. Will flood damage recur more frequently? And what about skiing? On the north-west shore of Lake Superior in Ontario, the ski season may be reduced by 30-40% over a century, with massive economic losses.

In Scotland, such predictions are not so readily available, and this is hardly surprising given the peculiarly intense interaction between the Atlantic Ocean and our atmosphere. In the Alps, the pessimistic forecasts point to the virtual wholescale elimination of alpine and higher zones from the central and southern European ranges – with only the Mount Blanc massif and the eastern Tyrol retaining these zones with approximately 150 specialist plants.

The frequency of very warm years will probably increase, and the rate of snowmelt will be greater. Adam Watson and co-researchers recently published evidence of some marked changes in the duration and lie of Scottish mountain snow patches – evidently related to variation in winter and spring weather.

It is still impossible to attach precision to impending changes. The already depleted remnants of arctic-alpine plant life must be at risk. Think of their adaptations to razor-sharp extremes in temperature, rain, snow and wind. Look at the snowbeds dazzling in the sunlight. If these melt progressively earlier and more quickly, belts of rare vegetation will be lost – possibly forever. By the year 2030 there may be just a few late-lying snowbeds in Scotland, with those in the south-west disappearing first.

The battle for our mountains, to protect their biodiversity and wildness, was started long ago – before the emergence of younger, better informed generations. But it is they who must rise to the calling of the mountains. It is between sheep and deer, people and their clutter, fire and rifles, and the ghostly passage of clouds and pollutants that we have to secure a better balance.

Many regions of the world have sacred and mystical elements of nature associated with their mountains. There, one finds degrees of reverence and protection not found in Scotland. Our mountains have an aura of spirituality, but not a corresponding degree of sanctity. The mountains deserve our best.

There is a land high in the mountains charged by
a magic not found elsewhere. This is the Lost World found
again. It is a timeless and lonely place, yet here the voice of silence
murmurs. Here can be the deadly elements – of gale and rain, cloud and
snow, and ridge and chasm – all cast by the dice of nature. There is a spell
of solitude when past and present, light and land transcend to mould that mood.

We are above the lower orders, far distant from the shires. I beseech you – rise above
these plains; come bide awhile in mossfool's world. Feel the heaths beneath your tread and
the ice-cold grip of rock. It is a fine thing to be in this place as part of such a world.

Say a prayer for the mountain and then descend. And as you dance and
weave on down, steal one last glimpse of where you were – now lost
again in the mist of time. It is in such a place as this that
kindred spirits touch – then pass.

Take Care In The Mountains

Mountains are among the most dangerous places on earth! The number of mountaineering deaths in Scotland has almost doubled over the last four years. During the period January-April 1994, 15 people died tragically in the mountains; in the same months of 1995, 22 died.

You should take great care at all times.

There are many excellent codes, pamphlets, books and magazines which deal with enjoyment and care in the mountains.

The guidance given below is taken mainly from codes prepared by members of the Mountaineering Council of Scotland and the Scottish Mountain Leadership Training Board, and issued to the public by the Scottish Sports Council.

Before you go

- Learn the use of map and compass
- Know the weather signs and heed local weather forecasts
- Plan within your capabilities
- Know simple first-aid and the symptoms of exposure
- Know the mountain distress signals
- Know the Country Code

When you go

- Wear climbing boots
- Do not go alone (unless you are very experienced)
- Leave written word of your route, and report your return
- Take windproofs, woollens and survival bag
- Take a map, compass and torch, and plenty of food
- Keep alert at all times

If there is much snow on the hills

- Always have an ice-axe for each person
- Carry a climbing rope and know the correct use of rope and ice-axe
- Learn to recognise dangerous snow slopes

Dangers and Hazards

Tracks and Paths

Part of Scotland's attraction lies in the wildness of its countryside. Few paths are signposted and even those clearly marked on maps may sometimes be difficult to trace. It is easy to follow a sheep or deer track which leads nowhere! Use your compass and check your location at all times.

Shelters and Stopping Points

Carry extra warm clothing and food supplies since you may not find a sheltered stopping point on your walk. Mountain shelters (bothies) are marked on the map but are not easy to locate; do not rely on these.

The Ground and Terrain

Scotland's varied terrain can make walking slow and exhausting. Rivers and burns can rise rapidly and become impassable. Consider these points when planning your walk, for they will affect the distance you can cover in the time available. Think about what could go wrong!

Limitations

Be aware of your own and your group's limitations (fitness, experience etc). If someone is tiring or cold, turn back. Do not allow a tired individual to return to base on his or her own.

Winter Snow
Even during summer months you may find patches of winter snow. Avoid these areas unless you have the skills to cope with the extra hazards. The snow will be hard, icy and very slippery. Remember, the majority of serious mountain accidents result from a simple slip or stumble.

The Weather
The changeable nature of the weather is one of the greatest hazards facing you in the mountains. Even on warm, sunny days bad weather can be upon you within an hour or so. If the wind strengthens, cloud thickens, visibility decreases or the temperature falls, turn back or find shelter. In poor visibility always use your map and compass.

Organisations

The Mountaineering Council of Scotland fosters mountaineering and promotes the interests of mountaineering clubs in Scotland. It co-operates with other bodies concerned with mountainous land, and works closely with the Scottish Countryside Activities Council, the Mountain Rescue Committee for Scotland, the Scottish Mountain Leadership Training Board and other countryside bodies. The Council is the voice of mountaineers in Scotland to central and local government, and to all others having responsibility for mountainous land. It works in partnership with the British Mountaineering Council.

Anyone wishing to approach mountaineering clubs, or indeed The Mountaineering Council of Scotland, should write first to the Honorary Secretary of the Mountaineering Council of Scotland, IR, 71 King Street, Crieff, Perthshire PH7 3HB, enclosing a stamped addressed envelope with your request.

The Scottish Sports Council is the official body concerned with the encouragement of sport and physical recreation amongst the general public in Scotland. It can be contacted at Caledonia House, South Gyle, Edinburgh EH12 9DQ.

THE JOHN MUIR TRUST

'Wildness is a necessity', as John Muir recognised over 100 years ago. We need to preserve wild places; not only rain forests and icecaps, but also Britain's own beautiful and diverse landscapes and wildlife.

In the Highlands and Islands of Scotland, Britain possesses one of Europe's finest wild land resources, yet this apparently unspoilt landscape shows everywhere the impact of its long human occupation, most notably in the loss of much of the great Caledonian pinewood. The process of degradation has accelerated in recent times, with overgrazing and blanket forestry, tracks bulldozed onto fragile mountain tops and hydro systems drowning beautiful glens.

Positive action is needed to halt this process of erosion and degradation. The John Muir Trust, formed in 1983, is committed to practical action to conserve Britain's remaining wild places, for their own sake, for the wildlife that depends on them, for the benefit of local communities and for the the enjoyment of future generations.

Already the Trust has bought four magnificent areas of wild land in Knoydart, in Skye and in north-west Sutherland – 35,000 acres in all. The most recent purchase was the Strathaird Estate in Skye, which includes the fine mountain of Bla Bheinn and adjoins the existing Trust land at Torrin. In partnership with local communities and other landowners the John Muir Trust is working to conserve these areas and to demonstrate what could be achieved for all our wild places.

The Trust is run by a board of Trustees and with only a small professional staff, is dependent on the enthusiasm and expertise of its members, who are spread throughout the country. With their assistance, the Trust will continue to build the necessary public support for wild land and to insist that we must leave for our children what we can of the beauty and biodiversity of our wild places.

For more information:,
JOHN MUIR TRUST, FREEPOST, Musselburgh, Midlothian, EH21 7BR

SCOTTISH NATURAL HERITAGE

Scottish Natural Heritage is a government agency established by Parliament in April 1992 and responsible to the Secretary of State for Scotland. It was formed by the merger of the Nature Conservancy Council for Scotland and the Countryside Commission for Scotland.

Its task is to secure the conservation and enhancement of Scotland's unique and precious natural heritage – habitats, landscapes and wildlife which have evolved through the long partnership between people and nature. SNH advises on policies and promotes projects which aim to improve the natural heritage and support its sustainable use. SNH's aim is to help people to enjoy Scotland's heritage responsibly, understand it more fully and use it wisely so that it can be sustained for future generations.

The aims of SNH are to:

- safeguard and enhance Scotland's natural heritage, particularly its genetic and scenic diversity;
- foster awareness and understanding of the natural heritage;
- encourage enjoyment of the natural heritage and promote responsible access to it, in a way which does not damage it;
- encourage public support and harness voluntary effort for the benefit of the environment;
- encourage environmental sustainability in all forms of economic development.

To achieve its objective, SNH works in a partnership with others, and has devolved a considerable measure of decision-making to the local level in order to be sensitive and accessible to local needs and circumstances.

Mountains and SNH

Many of SNH's activities are concerned with Scotland's mountain country. Much effort has to be devoted to the protection and management of statutory sites such as Sites of Special Scientific Interest, as well as National Scenic Areas.

Red Deer and the Natural Heritage

In 1994 SNH published a policy and action paper on this key issue. Working closely with the Red Deer Commission and deer estate owners and managers, SNH seeks to develop Management Plans for each of the Deer Management Group areas and to set up demonstrations of positive action on land.

Access and Enjoyment

Also in 1994, SNH published a policy and action paper, Enjoying the Outdoors, which sets out an ambitious agenda for fostering more responsible enjoyment in mountain country. There have been many long-standing conflicts between recreationists and land managers connected with sporting, agricultural and other activities, but these are gradually being resolved. SNH supports the maintenance of Long Distance Routes such as the Southern Upland Way and West Highland Way, and is promoting a 'Paths for All' initiative designed to provide networks of small paths round settlements.

National Nature Reserve Management

Several of SNH's largest upland NNRs are managed to demonstrate how to bring benefit to the natural heritage. Rum, Creag Meagaidh, Beinn Eighe and Inchrory have major programmes of woodland regeneration. Some NNRs are managed in partnership with other bodies: Ben Lawers with the National Trust for Scotland to enhance remnant plant communities, and the Muir of Dinnet with the owner to display moorland and birch woodland at their best.

Education and Publicity

SNH conducts a range of activities to promote awareness of the mountains. There are many school and university projects, and some Field Centres, such as Knockan in Assynt, provide major interpretations of key areas, features and processes. Many books, reports, pamphlets, and advisory schedules are available from the SNH Communications Directorate.

Research and Advice

Much remains to be discovered about our mountain ecosystems and landscapes. SNH commissions research to fill gaps in our knowledge, such as: survey of important geological features, landforms, species, communities and indeed users of the land; work to determine animal and plant populations and their habitat requirements; and measures to improve land management. Some of this is done nationally, but much is done at the local area level. Most of the findings are published in reports as well as in the form of advisory notes – making the results and lessons to be learned readily available.

The Cairngorms, and the Trossachs

The Secretary of State for Scotland responded to the report of the Cairngroms Working Party in November 1994. SNH is providing resources, information and advice (much of it based on new reserach and inventory work) to support the Cairngorms Partnership Board in pursuing the priorities set by government. Comparable effort is also being devoted to Loch Lomond and the Trossachs.

Natura 2000

SNH is responsible for the identification of Special Protection Areas and Special Areas for Conservation (collectively called Natura 2000 sites under the European Birds and Habitats Directives). Many of the largest sites embrace mountain habitats and wildlife, and these will be monitored to ensure that favourable conservation status is maintained.

UK Biodiversity Action Plan

Following the Rio Conference, Government is preparing habitat and species Action Plans. SNH is taking the lead in implementing these in Scotland, not least through high profile 'species recovery' programmes in places such as Ben Lawers, the Cairngorms and Ben Alder.

Objective 1 Projects

Liverpool and the Highlands and Islands qualify in Britain for EU 'Objective 1' funding – to build up the local economy in areas of acute economic difficulty. The Objective 1 plan for the Highlands and Islands emphasises the environmental importance of the area, and SNH plays a key role in shaping the plan. For example, SNH is involved in footpath restoration on Sgurr nan Gillean and in supporting the new Ferry Croft Visitor Centre near Lairg.

SNH addresses:
Main HQ : 12 Hope Terrace, Edinburgh, EH9 2AS

Communications Directorate (Publications, Education, Training, Interpretation): Battleby, Redgorton, Perth, PH1 3EW

Research and Advisory Services Directorate: 2 Anderson Place, Edinburgh, EH6 5NP

NW Region: Fraser Darling House, 9 Culduthel Road, Inverness, IV2 4AG (also four area offices)

NE Region: Wynne-Edwards House, 17 Rubislaw Terrace, Aberdeen, AB1 1XE (also three area offices)

SW Region: Caspian House, Mariner Court, Clydebank Business Park, Clydebank, G81 2NR (also three area offices)

SE Region: Battleby, Redgorton, Perth, PH1 3EW (also three area offices)

SNH produces a quarterly magazine, *Scotland's Natural Heritage*, available on request from the Communications Directorate

Bibiliography

Baird, W.J. (1988) *The Scenery of Scotland*. Edinburgh: National Museums of Scotland.

Ballantyne, C.K. (1991) Holocene geomorphic activity in the Scottish Highlands. *Scottish Geographical Magazine*, 107: 84-98.

Ballantyne, C.K. & Harris, C. (1994) *The Periglaciation of Great Britain*. Cambridge: Cambridge University Press.

Barry, R.G. (1981) *Mountain Weather and Climate*. London: Methuen.

Baxter, C. & Goodier, R. (1990) *The Cairngorms*. Lanark: Colin Baxter Photography.

Bennet, D. (Ed.) (1986) *The Munros*. The Scottish Mountaineering Club Hillwalkers' Guide. Glasgow: The Scottish Mountaineering Trust.

Bennet, D.J. & Strang, T. (1990) *The Northwest Highlands*. Glasgow: Scottish Mountaineering Trust.

Benston, M. (Ed.) (1994) *Mountain Environments in Changing Climates*. London: Routledge.

Birks, H.J.B. (1973) *Past and Present Vegetation of the Isle of Skye - a Palaeoecological Study*. Cambridge: Cambridge University Press.

Bonington, Chris (Ed.) (1994) *Great Climbs*. London: Mitchell Beazley.

Boyd, J.M. & Boyd, I.L. (1990) *The Hebrides: a natural history*. London: Collins.

Brockie, K. (1993) *Mountain Reflections*. Edinburgh: Mainstream.

Brown, A., Birks, H.J.B. & Thompson, D.B.A. (1993) A new biogeographical classification of the Scottish uplands. II. Vegetation-environment relationships. *Journal of Ecology*, 81:231-251.

Brown, H. (ed.) (1982) *Poems of the Scottish Hills*. Aberdeen: Aberdeen University Press.

Browne, M. & Mendum, J. (1995) *Loch Lomond to Stirling*. Battleby: Scottish Natural Heritage.

Butterfield, I. (1993) *The High Mountains of Britain and Ireland*. London: Diadem.

Cairngorms Working Party (1993) *Common Sense and Sustainability: A Partnership for the Cairngorms*. Edinburgh: The Scottish Office (HMSO).

Clutton-Brock, T.H. & Albon, S.D. (1989) *Red Deer in the Highlands*. Oxford: Blackwell Scientific Publications.

CM2428 (1994) *The UK Biodiversity Action Plan*. Command 2428. London: HMSO.

Conroy, J.W.H., Watson, A. & Gunson, A.R. (eds.) (1990) 'Caring for the High Mountains.' Proceedings of the conference on conservation of the Cairngorms. Aberdeen: Centre for Scottish Studies and Natural Environment Research Council.

Countryside Commission for Scotland (1990) *The Mountain Areas of Scotland*. Perth: Countryside Commission for Scotland.

Craig, G.Y. (1991) *Geology of Scotland*. Fourth edition. London: The Geological Society.

Crawford, B.E. (1987) *Scandinavian Scotland*. Leicester: Leicester University Press.

Crofts, R. (1995) 'The Environment – Who Cares?' Occasional Paper No.2. Battleby: Scottish Natural Heritage.

Crumley, J. (1991) *A High and Lonely Place. The Sanctuary and Plight of the Cairngorms*. London: Jonathan Cape.

Crumley, J. (1994) *Among Mountains*. London: Mainstream.

Curry-Lindahl, K., Watson, A. & Watson, R. (1988) *The Future of the Cairngorms*. Aberdeen: North East Mountain Trust.

Darling, F. F. (1947) *Natural History in the Highlands and Islands*. London: Collins

Darling, F.F. (1955) *West Highland Survey: An Essay in Human Ecology*. Oxford: Oxford University Press.

Darling, F.F. & Boyd, J.M. (1964) *The Highlands and Islands*. London: Collins.

Darling, F.F. (1969) *Wilderness and Plenty: The Reith Lectures 1969*. London: BBC.

Defoe, D. (1726) *Tour Through the Whole Island of Great Britain*

Dickson, J.H. (1993) Scottish woodlands: their ancient past and precarious future. *Botanical Journal of Scotland*, 26.

Everett, R. (Ed.) (1993) *Northern Highlands Rock and Ice Climbs. Vol 2. Strathfarrar to Shetland*. Edinburgh: Scottish Mountaineering Trust.

Gerrard, J. (1990) *Mountain Environments*. London: Belhaven.

Gerrard, J. (1991) Mountains under pressure. *Scottish Geographical Magazine*, 107: 75-83.

Gilbert, R. (1983) *Memorable Munros*. Leicester: Diadem.

Gordon, J., Brazier, V., Keast, S. & Threadgould, R. (1994) *Cairngorms. A Landscape Fashioned by Geology*. Battleby: Scottish Natural Heritage.

Gordon, J.E. & Sutherland, D.G. (eds.) (1993) 'Quaternary of Scotland.' *Geological Conservation Review* Series 6. London: Chapman & Hall.

Gordon, J.E., Taylor, A. & Usher, M.B. (eds.) (1995) *Soils, Sustainability and the Natural Heritage*. Edinburgh: HMSO.

Gordon, S. (1935) *Highways and Byways in the West Highlands*. London: Macmillan.

Gordon, S. (1955) *The Golden Eagle. King of Birds*. London: Collins.

Grieve, I.C., Hipkin, J.A. & Davidson, D.A. (1994) 'Soil erosion sensitivity in upland Scotland. Research,' Survey and Monitoring Report No. 24. Battleby: Scottish Natural Heritage.

Hunt, J. & Wilkinson, M. (1995) *Ross and Cromarty Upland Footpath Survey. Economy and Use*. Dingwall: Ross and Cromarty Enterprise and Scottish Natural Heritage.

IUCN (International Union for Conservation of Nature and Natural Resources) (1994) *Parks for Life. Action for Protected Areas in Europe*. London: IUCN.

Ives, J.D. & Messerli, B. (1990) Progress in theoretical and applied mountain research, 1973-1989, and future needs. *Mountain Research and Development*,10: 101-127.

Johnson, S. & Boswell, J. (1775 and 1785) *A Journey to the Western Islands of Scotland* and *The Journal of a Tour to the Hebrides* (edited by R.W. Chapman) 1924. Oxford: Oxford University Press.

Johnstone, S., Brown, H. & Bennet, D. (Eds) (1990) 'The Corbetts and other Scottish Hills.' *Scottish Mountaineering Club Hillwalkers Guide*, Volume 2. Glasgow: Scottish Mountaineering Trust.

Lamb, H.H. (1982) *Climate, History and the Modern World*. London: Methven.

Langmuir, E. (1990) *Mountaincraft and Leadership. Handbook of the Scottish Mountaineering Leadership Training Board*. Edinburgh: Scottish Sports Council.

Lister-Kaye, J. (1994) 'Ill Fares the Land. A Sustainable Land Ethic for Sporting Estates of the Highlands and Islands of Scotland.' Occasional Paper No.3. Battleby: Scottish Natural Heritage.

Loch Lomond and Trossachs Working Party (1993) *The Management of Loch Lomond and The Trossachs*. Edinburgh: The Scottish Office (HMSO).

Macdonald, A. & P. (1992) *Granite and Green.Above North-East Scotland*. London: Mainstream.

Mackenzie, O. (1924) *A Hundred Years in the Highlands*. London: Arnold.

Manley, G. (1952) *Climate and the British Scene*. London: Collins.

Magnusson, M. (1993) Red deer and Scotland's natural heritage. *Deer*, 9:19-22.

Magnusson, M. & White, G. (Eds) (1991) *The Nature of Scotland. Landscape, Wildlife and People*. Edinburgh: Canongate.

McConnochie, A. (1923) *The Deer and Deer Forests of Scotland*. London: Witherby.

McLean, A.C. (1976) *Explore the Highlands and Islands*. Inverness: Highlands and Islands Development Board.

McNeish, C. (1991) *The Munro Almanac*. Moffat: Lochar.

McNeish, C. (1994) *The Corbett Almanac*. Glasgow: Neil Wilson.

McNeish, C. & Else, R. (1994) *The Edge.One hundred years of Scottish mountaineering*. London: BBC Books.

McVean, D.N. & Lockie, J.D. (1969) *Ecology and Land-use in Upland Scotland*. Edinburgh: Edinburgh University Press.